WHO HAS NOT experienced the eerie feeling, on glimpsing a village street or foreign seaport, that he has been there before? Who has not met a stranger with whom he felt instant rapport, as if he had always known him, or taken a violent dislike to another before the introductions were even completed? Could these inner stirrings perhaps be prompted by soul memories of past life encounters?

READ
Here and Hereafter
THEN ASK YOURSELF:

*Is the cycle of rebirth
really so hard to believe?*

HERE AND HEREAFTER

Ruth Montgomery

FAWCETT CREST • NEW YORK

Contents

Foreword

IN our present state of development, it is no more possible to prove reincarnation than to prove the existence of God. But the doctrine of karma and rebirth is so logical that if two-thirds of the world's peoples did not already accept it, it would probably be hailed by We_terners today as a major philosophical breakthrough. The belief is older than recorded history, having been handed down by word of mouth until man learned to record his thoughts in hieroglyphics. It explains, better than does any one known creed, why some are born to affluence and others to abject poverty. Why one youngster is a genius and another a dullard. Why some are criprled o⁻ blind; others healthy and beautiful.

The Old Testament teaches "An eye for an eye, a tooth for a tooth," yet we need look no farther than our own neighborhood to observe that sin often goes unpunished here, while greed is seemingly rewarded. Only when one acce⁻ts the thesis that we have existed since the beginning of time, and that what a man sows in one lifetime will be reaped in subsequent ones does the Biblical injunction make sense. A major tenet of Brahmanism was stated long ago in the Bhagavad-Gita: "As a man, casting off worn-out garments, taketh new ones, so the dweller in the body, casting off worn-out bodies, entereth into others that are new. For sure is the death of him that is born, and sure the birth of him that is dead; therefore over the inevitable thou shouldst not grieve."

Six centuries before the birth of Jesus, Gautama Buddha taught that there is no escaping the result of man's actions; that without the cycle of rebirth life is meaningless and without purpose. Buddhists, like Brahmans, strive for emancipation from the cycle of return, which is considered possible only after man has achieved such perfection that he can earn nirvana, or oneness with God. This yearning may help to explain an otherwise abstruse passage in Revelations III:12: "Him that overcometh will I make a pillar in the temple of my God, and he shall go no more out."

The Essenes, a Jewish sect considered by numerous scholars to have been the teachers of John the Baptist and Jesus, believed in reincarnation, and early Christians accepted the doctrine as a matter of course. When Jesus asked His disciples who men thought He was, they replied: "Some say that Thou art John the Baptist; some, Elias; and others, Jeremiah, or one of the prophets." In Matthew 17:9-13 we read that after the disciples questioned Jesus about the Old Testament prophecy that Elias "must first come" before the Savior, He replied: "Elias truly shall first come, and restore all things. But I say unto you, that Elias is come already, and they knew him not, but have done unto him whatsoever they listed. Likewise shall also the Son of man suffer of them."

"Then," it adds, "the disciples understood that He spake unto them of John the Baptist," who had been beheaded by Herod.

Belief in reincarnation persisted in the early Christian church for several centuries. In the Confessions of St. Augustine 1:6 we read:"Did I not live in another body, or somewhere else, before entering my mother's womb?" The apocryphal book Pistis Sophia, which some claim to be the esoteric teachings of Jesus to Mary Magdalene, records: "But if he shall have sinned once, twice, or thrice, they shall reject that soul sending it back again into the world according to the form of the sin that it may have committed."

In the sixth century the Synod of Constantinople (which was not attended by the Pope of Rome) condemned the teaching of reincarnation, and some scholars believe that most references to it were thereupon expunged from the Bible, but among leading Catholic theologians who advocated the philosophy during the Middle Ages were St. Francis of

Assisi, founder of the Franciscan Order; the Irish monk, Johannes Scotus Erigena; and the Dominican monk, Thomas Campanella. In more recent times Cardinal Mercier, prelate of Belgian Catholics, stated that the doctrine in no way conflicts with Catholic dogma; and Dean Inge of St. Paul's Cathedral in London declared: "I find the doctrine [of reincarnation] both credible and attractive."

François Marie Voltaire, the satirical French philosopher, observed that "it is not more surprising to be born twice than once," and such diverse New World personalities as Benjamin Franklin, Ralph Waldo Emerson, Henry Ford and Thomas Edison espoused the belief.

But if we have lived before, why can we not remember it? Actually, many seemingly do. Who has not experienced the eerie feeling, on glimpsing a village street or foreign seaport, that he has been there before? Who has not found himself in a situation which seems startlingly familiar, although his reason tells him otherwise? Who has not met a stranger with whom he felt instant rapport, as if he had always known him; or taken a violent dislike to another before the introductions were even completed? Could these inner stirrings perhaps be prompted by soul memories of past life encounters?

Newspapers and books have recorded innumerable instances of small children who insist that they used to be someone else, and who vividly describe a lifetime in a locale that they have never visited. These prattlings could be written off as flights of fancy, were it not that many of the people and places named, and the happenings that they recount have subsequently been verified by disinterested investigators.

Some people, while lacking these instantaneous flashes, have trained themselves through meditation or dreams to recapture memories which seem to stem from previous earthly sojourns. Numerous others while under hypnosis have recalled authenticated happenings of their babyhood, and then continued to regress until they were detailing events which they claim occurred in previous incarnations, although they possess no conscious knowlege of the places. Some even speak in foreign languages that are unknown to them. Still others have been told of previous lifetimes by psychics who were in trance.

But does it matter whether we have lived before? Yes, because if this is not our first lifetime it will probably not be our last, and we consequently have it within our power to influence our future circumstances by present conduct. If all of us could accept the philosophy that life is a continuing force, and that what we do to others now will be done to us in future incarnations, our behavior would dramatically improve. Who would want to cheat a business associate or steal another's spouse if he believed that by such conduct he would be damaging his own chances for happiness in a subsequent life on earth?

Is God so whimsical and unloving that He plays favorites with His children, granting radiant health to one and misery to another, or does the explanation for this seeming inequality lie within each of us? If we accept the philosophy of reincarnation and karma, we can see ourselves as in a mirror—knowing that we are what we have been, and that we will become what we are now, unless we drastically mend our ways. Such a tenet, firmly held, could revolutionize this strife-torn world.

This is a book about people living today, many of whom for the first time are permitting their names to be used in connection with personal experiences which seem to suggest that they have lived many times before. The purpose of the book is to emphasize the deep spiritual values to be derived from knowing oneself; for if man chose to be reborn in order to right previously committed wrongs and strive for perfection of spirit, the recapturing of soul memories could assist him in discovering the mission which was his prenatal goal.

Who would resent his bodily imperfections, if he understood that by deliberately selecting them and cheerfully coping with the self-imposed handicap he is freeing his soul of more serious blemishes? Would a man riot because he was born into poverty, if he believed that he himself had volunteered for that lowly situation in order to learn the needed lesson of humility? Would another be arrogant and smug if he knew that he had selected a life of wealth in order to test his own qualities of compassion and generosity?

Some of the people who are discussed in this book gave their permission reluctantly, but with the awareness that unless each of us has the courage to stand up and be counted, research into man's knowledge of himself will continue to lag behind scientific advances in other less vital fields. Mrs. Wilfred (Elsie) Sechrist does not claim as "fact" that she died of tuberculosis while married to a famous artist, nor does the Reverend George Emery seek to "prove" that his soul once inhabited the physical body of an eighteenth-century English evangelist. Hugh Lynn Cayce has no legal evidence that he was a Crusader in one lifetime, and a Norse conqueror in another. Was Dr. Stanley Krippner personally present at the court of Kublai Khan, or was it his imagination? He does not even pretend to know; but these outstanding, well-educated Americans are sufficiently interested in the philosophy of reincarnation to disclose their psychic experiences, hoping that when fitted into the larger mosaic, these isolated fragments may help to solve the riddle of life.

Who am I? We are the sum total of all our experiences. If born again, whom will I become? With each thought, word, and deed we are presently constructing the person that we will be. It is an awesome thought.

I

How to Remember

INSOFAR as I can recall, the first time that I experienced a strong sensation of familiarity with a strange place occurred in 1952, while on a news-gathering assignment in the Middle East. The Egyptian Foreign Office had provided a guide, and at my request we made our initial stop at the Great Pyramid in Giza, whose peak I had excitedly glimpsed from the balcony of my Nile-side room, at the Semiramis Hotel in Cairo. A comfortable feeling of "belonging" swept over me as we approached the pyramid, and when we stood at the entrance, the guide began, "We have to stoop our heads and proceed along a narrow passageway for about . . ."

"Yes," I interrupted. "Then we bear right and upward, and then . . ." and gave the remaining directions for reaching the king's chamber.

The guide started in surprise, saying, "But I thought you said this was you first visit to Egypt."

"It is," I replied, and added shakily, "but I've been in that pyramid before."

I did not consciously believe it, nor could I understand why I had made such a spontaneous remark. I had never given any particular thought to reincarnation, and if someone had told me that he believed in it, I would have laughed him off as a freak. Yet, as we inched our way along the dark passages, aided only by the flickering light of a candle, each turn was precisely as I had indicated. It was impossible that I could somewhere have read such directions, because although pictures of the pyramids were naturally familiar, I knew so little about them that I had assumed them to be virtually hollow structures. In the years since, I have repeatedly been drawn back to Egypt, choosing to go there rather than to places I have not yet visited, or to more glamorous spots that I have known. Each time, I am again seized by that odd feeling of belonging. The Nile seems as familiar to me as the Potomac, on whose banks I have lived for a quarter century. I am shamefully lax in remembering names and faces, but I never forget an Egyptian one. On subsequent trips, I have felt so at home in Luxor and the Temple of Karnak that I could scarcely bear to leave.

A similar sense of "returning home" overwhelmed me in Palestine, particularly at the site of Capernaum on the Sea of Galilee, and in the Dead Sea area near Jericho. It was as if I had trod those paths many times before, although such a reaction may be a normal outgrowth of religious emotions.

Even after I began delving into psychic phenomena, the subject of reincarnation failed to stir my interest. My initial skepticism about the possibility of communication between the living and the so-called dead had gradually dissolved, in the face of mounting evidence; but to believe that each of us has survived many previous deaths, and will emerge again from a mother's womb, seemed to belie reason. Then, toward the end of my work on *A Search for the Truth* in 1965, the mysterious Guides who had been bringing messages through automatic writing began to hint at reincarnation, in this manner:

"We are no more the 'hereafter' than you are, who sprang from a previous stage which you cannot recall. The very thought that thinking human beings sprang fully developed in that one state of existence would seem laughable to any except you earth people, who are accustomed to accepting everything at face value. You who are more advanced and sensitive have lived through many previous phases, while some of the more doltish varieties had only primer training in a previous step. To that life which went before, you are as much the 'hereafter' as we here are to you. The hereafter goes on and on, my dear child, until at last you and we and all of us eventually pass through that Golden Door where longing shall be no more, where perfection has been attained, and where we are at last one with God, our Creator. This voyage through the various stages of life can be as rapidly performed, or as slowly drawn, as you make it, depending on your own contribution there, here, and in all the various steps. The progress depends on you, not on God, Who has given all equal opportunity, although not all have the same opportunity at each level of their advancement."

The Guides added that since some are in different stages of living than others, "The ones you call the 'unfortunate' may not be unfortunate at all. It may simply be their way of achieving goodness and oneness with God more rapidly than you, because if they sacrifice more, and live more abundantly for others, they are far more fortunate than those of you with mink coats, chauffeured cars, and the countless temptations that beset your trail through the maze of parties and working hours."

Several weeks later, they wrote: "Those who feel that they have lived before are not too far off base. The thing they misunderstand is that no personality is completely reborn. As the soul advances, the baser parts are sluffed off as a shell, and the shining parts blossom into new heights. As a consequence, no one is the same person he would have been in an earlier existence, or has lived before in the recognizable form of personality that now exists. The growth of the soul so advances and polishes personality, that were we to be reincarnated we would not seem to those who knew us to be the same entity as before. Parts of us remain, but not the whole man who sinned and struggled and loved and slaved. We here are not the same entity in its entirety that we were in our earth-life. We have memories and knowledge acquired during that phase, but we are constantly progressing, so that the less important things of the earth are now forgotten by us." Another time, they wrote: "We were first born in God. God is our ultimate home. It is the cycle of the universe, to seek that of which we once were a glowing part. Our reunion with God will be the ultimate step by which we will obtain the glory of true love and happiness . . . but we have millenniums yet to go in our progression toward eternal truth and Oneness with God."

After the publication of *A Search for the Truth*, a number of editors contacted me about writing books for them, and I was giving serious consideration to one about Washington,

D.C., when the Guides began urging me to tackle the subject of reincarnation, declaring: "We will now discuss the path that a soul follows from its original breath of life until its reunion with the Creator. To understand the beginnings, picture a revolving sun, brilliant, warm and enveloping, which sprays off fragments of itself in its rapid evolutions. Each is a tiny little light that has set forth upon its way through darkness, with but one goal in mind, to rejoin the sun from which it sprang. But as the little sparklets take on the breath of life granted by their Creator, they turn this way and that, eager to see what may lie in the darkness, but also afraid; so that instead of helping to guide other little lost sparks back toward the radiant center, they may hide for a time, or become so engrossed in themselves returning that they forget to administer to other lost sparks. This is simply a pictorial illustration, and is not meant to signify that God is practically the sun. It might be misunderstood unless we here explain that the sun, like all the other planets and stars and satellites, is merely another manifestation of God's universe from whence we all sprang eons ago, but the journey ends when we at last achieve such understanding of God's will and such perfection of soul that we are fit to rejoin God. Try to understand that as we return again and again to earth to complete our purification, we are beset not only by the old sins that we came to resolve, but also by new temptations which must be met and overcome, or we do not grow."

At another session, the Guides emphasized that we not only choose to be reborn, but also have free will in working off previously incurred karma. "There is no set pattern," they declared, "which decrees that at such and such a time we will meet a situation which will permit us to dissolve the age-old scar on our akashic record of all thought forms and experiences of mankind. We make our own opportunities, and although we may have returned to dispel certain karma, we will wisely work off other debts until the time comes when we are able to dispel the one we particularly wished to cancel out. It will thus be seen that every minute counts, and no time should be wasted; for the more rapidly we repay these debts the sooner we will be freed from the wheel of recurring earth lives, and advance to higher dimensions. Remember not to acquire habits and yens that bind you too closely to the earth, for they invariably keep you coming back there, rather than growing here in wisdom and spirituality."

The Guides, reminding that many millions of people have believed in reincarnation "since time immemorial," directed attention to what they termed "the wrong attitude of many Orientals, who try to escape the eternal wheel by withdrawing from life and living one of pure contemplation." This, they said, "defeats the very purpose of rebirth, for instead of helping others and doing all possible to make a real contribution to the betterment of mankind, they withdraw into themselves, thinking of their own salvation rather than helping others to achieve it." They added that "this listless attitude has caused great harm among the backward peoples, who would benefit greatly by the keen minds and brilliant thought processes of the seers and yogis who should devote themselves to the people, rather than to their own quest for nirvana."

The Guides declared that it is sometimes possible for a soul to work off bad karma without reincarnating, "if there is not too much of it," by helping those on the earth plane to progress. "By so doing we gradually, oh so gradually, progress to higher stages here," they continued. "But some unfortunately lack the patience to work out their salvation here, or have incurred so much indebtedness there that it is almost impossible to repay the obligations here. Thus, after staying here long enough to realize the enormity of his error, a soul will deliberately choose to reincarnate for faster progress, and through hardships of the earth phase to repay some of the damage he has done there."

Then they wrote this intriguing passage: "Some plunge back into earthly forms too quickly to realize the purpose of reincarnation. Thus, they lack the detachment and wisdom to improve their own lot, or that of others. They are strictly earth people, not Old Souls, and it is these who cause so much of the strife and discord there, for they lack the broad view and tolerance for others." Referring to soldiers "who became victims of their nation's national policy and died in battle," the Guides said that inasmuch as they were "cheated out of their earth phase by events not of their own making," they are often the first to be reborn. "Some stay awhile to recover their quietude and seek to communicate with loved ones on the earth plane, but others plunge back rapidly into another fetus or newborn baby before they have learned the all-powerful weapon for good, the power of love.

"Often these soldiers and others who are accidentally killed in the fighting reincarnate within weeks of the crossover," the

Guides continued. "They carry back with them burning resentment against a war which robbed them of life in their youth, and disdain for older people who forced them into such a situation through war. These are the ones most likely to lead the revolts, the student uprisings, the loudly expressed criticism of elders; storming against the policy in Vietnam or anywhere else that leads to the killing of youth, and against the conscription that would force them to kill others. It is understandable that they feel this revolt within themselves, but they do not know why. If they understood the reason for their burning zeal against war, they might take a more philosophical and thoughtful approach, forming councils or study groups to work with the older generation to defeat policies that eventually lead to war, rather than aimlessly and loudly protesting, without solutions."

Inasmuch as the Bible warns of "an eye for an eye," I asked how this admonition applies to servicemen who are required to kill the enemy in battle. The Guides replied: "This question is not as perplexing as it seems at first glance. Those who, in the name of protecting their country, are forced to slay those whom their nation has branded 'enemy' have no responsibility for an act which is committed according to man-made laws, and for which the man has no lust or liking. But the ones who go beyond the call of duty by relishing the slaying, and who inflict torture merely for torture's sake—not because they are commanded to do so by a superior in order to exact knowledge from the prisoner—must pay the same penalty as a civilian who tortures or murders fellow human beings. The difference, then, stems from the heart of the individual soldier. If ordered to kill in order to save his nation or a segment of humanity, or because his government has ordered him to be a brave soldier and go into battle, he will bear no scars for the slaughter; but he must never relish killing, and must not torture captives unless bade to do so for a purpose."

Intrigued by these messages from an unknown source, I began to study the subject of reincarnation, including the life readings given by Edgar Cayce, and innumerable books on the subject. Surprised to learn that many people were seemingly able to recapture detailed memories of past lives, I asked the Guides how others might do likewise, and they wrote: "When you think back to certain aspects of your childhood which stand out as unique, see if you will remember something else that seemed to have promulgated that situation for which there seemed no explanation. This could help to remind you of something in a previous earth phase that was influencing you in this one. These happenings are the best for recollections of earlier lives, before you become too immersed in this one. Muse on those childhood events which most stand out in memory; then try to determine why they impressed you so much more than others."

At a later date, they wrote: "The easiest way to prompt one's faulty memory is by reaching back into the mind through meditation. Then, as the glimmers of truth flash before the inner eye, one may seek to determine from whence they came. As a starter, one could simply recall a past experience which made an unusual impact, such as a doorway that seemed familiar, the tantalizing aroma of a flower not previously encountered, or the yearning for a particular fragrance or taste. Your own love of licorice means that you once lived in the East, where you were addicted to anise. Why do you love butter beans so much? Because you once cultivated them in another life. You nursed them, loved to watch them develop, and considered them the most beautiful plant in your world; and before we knew so much about nutrition, you had convinced yourself that the richness of flavor and solid quality must make butter beans the most nourishing and sustaining food in the world. This was when you ate no meat, and lived virtually as a hermit; but this is only a sample of what each person will be able to do, in drawing forth the influences that made him what he is today."

The following week, the Guides sought to be more specific in their suggestions for recapturing memories. They proposed that we let the mind roam backward to a place which we feel that we have visited before, to a surrounding in which we have felt as comfortable as if it were home, or to a situation which we seemed to have lived through before. Then we should try to analyze the feeling. Why was it so familiar? Had we dreamed it, or visited a similar place? If not, we should make notes of the conditions, and keep a running diary of these recollections, matching each notation with comments on the circumstances and the perceptive flashes until, like pieces of a jigsaw, they begin to form patterns. Soon, the Guides declared, a flash of total recall may occur, so that a previous incarnation is suddenly revealed to us. At that point, they said, we should analyze each fragment of that life, to see what has influenced our present course of action, what errors of commission or omission we are here to rectify, and what good we accomplished from which we are now reaping benefit.

Another day, they wrote: "Those who would recall past lives should keep a notebook on incidents which are hard to explain by ordinary intellect. These would include happenings of the past that bore no relationship to one's conscious awareness or intellect at the time, dreams that were unrelated to everyday happenings, memories stirred by a place visited which had not previously been seen by one's physical eyes, recognition of someone who had until then been a stranger, strong affinity for persons, places, things, tastes and smells, fear unprompted by remembered events, or happiness unrelated to known causes. Keep a running list, and space for comment beside each such recall; then meditate separately on these isolated incidents. Visualize oneself in another time and place, trying to fit it into the mosaic of fragmented recall. Isolate each incident as to time, place and sensory reaction; then see if it will drop into the jigsaw of past incarnation."

Subsequently, they elaborated: "Begin each day to meditate on one childhood experience or reaction at a time, trying to relax and take it with you into the recesses of the subconscious, so that outcroppings of previous lives are stirred. At bedtime, concentrate briefly on the same incident that you have used in meditation, and let the mind of the unconscious work over it while you sleep. Keep pencil and pad beside the bed, and plan to jot down these flashes of recall as you awaken."

Since publication of *A Search for the Truth*, many readers have written to ask whether I yet know the identity of the principal Guide who identifies himself by drawing a flower beside the word Lily if a pencil is being used. I still do not. Some have suggested that the messages, rather than originating with an entity who is no longer in physical body, may stem from my own subconscious; others believe that I am tapping into my "higher self," or superconsciousness. I have no way of knowing, except to be convinced that the philosophy contained was not previously in my conscious thought.

I would be willing to accept the "higher self," or "superconscious," explanation, were it not for a strange series of happenings early in 1967. Olga Worrall, the famous Baltimore psychic who, with her husband Ambrose, coauthored the excellent bok, *The Gift of Healing,* had given me a copy of it. I therefore sent her an advance copy of *A Search for the Truth,* before it appeared in bookstores, and on January 31, 1967, she wrote to say how much she was enjoying it. At the lower left-hand corner of her letter she had drawn a picture of a flower, and written "Lily" beside it. I was astonished! Although I had shown no one the automatic writing, this was precisely the way Lily himself drew a flower and signed his name, all in one sweep of the pencil.

I wrote to her of my surprise, and illustrated what I meant by sketching the way I think a lily should be drawn; for Lily's flower looks like a six-petaled daisy with a two-leafed tulip stem, and that is the way Mrs. Worrall had drawn hers, even to the same number of petals and leaves. On February fifth, I received a reply from Mrs. Worrall which said, "As I ended that letter to you, your Lily appeared to me (and I can assure you that he wasn't in my thoughts) and said he wanted me to add his signature. Needless to say I was startled. Without thinking, I found myself drawing a lily that looked very unlilylike—but Lily insisted that it was what he wanted. I majored in art in school and I really do know how a lily should be drawn, but your Lily had other ideas. When Ambrose read my letter to you he commented on the silly-looking lily, and I found myself telling him, 'I can't redraw it, but Ruth will understand.' Things like this can't be explained. I am really thrilled over Lily's signature, because this verifies what you have been receiving from him. He is 'for real.' "

What Mrs. Worrall did not know was that three hours before the postman delivered to me her second letter, I sat for my regular automatic writing session, which began like this: "Ruth, this is Lily. The way Mrs. Worrall drew my signature was because we showed it to her as further proof to you that we are here and able to communicate, that it is not your subconscious or another part of your mind. This she will tell you soon."

At that time I had not, of course, heard again from Mrs. Worrall, and consequently had no idea that she had "seen" Lily, or been told by him to draw the lily in that fashion. Yet her letter, written to me the day before Lily wrote the above, contained the message that he said I would receive from her: that he is "real," rather than a part of my own super- or subconscious.

II

Inner Promptings

THE inner turmoil and physical torments of a deathbed scene more than a century ago were seemingly relived by a prominent psychiatrist in Chicago, who is world-famous for his work in the field of dream interpretation, but who for professional reasons asks that he merely be called Dr. Smith. The dramatic experience occurred at the home of Dr. and Mrs. Denys Kelsey, in the south of France, during the summer of 1967. Dr. Smith, while in a semihypnotic state induced by Dr. Kelsey, "recalled" a German incarnation in the early Victorian era, as a young woman who gave rather freely of her love. After a particularly unhappy love affair, she married a wealthy German and thereafter swung to the opposite extreme, becoming so self-righteous and prim that she was exceedingly intolerant of others' improprieties. Concealing her own youthful indiscretions from family and friends, the straitlaced matriarch ruled her children with a will of iron; but despite her high social position she was unhappy, secretly yearning for the warm and loving part of her nature that she had ruthlessly suppressed.

Dr. Smith's most vivid recollection of that lifetime was its final moments, when in her late seventies the woman lay dying of cancer of the lower intestines. As a staunch Roman Catholic, she was confronted with a nearly insurmountable problem. One of her sons was her priest-confessor, and as her family surrounded the bed, while he prepared to administer the last rites of the Church, she was caught in a bitter dilemma: how to rid her soul of sin by confessing her long-held secrets, without exposing them to her own children.

Dr. Smith says that he actually experienced the woman's physical as well as emotional anguish while she wrestled with her conscience, and he believes that the traumatic experience of that incarnation may have influenced his present lifetime. With a rueful smile he explains, "I deplore that in my Chicago youth, I was so proper and inhibited in my attitudes that I missed many opportunities for pleasant social activities, and my first marital venture proved unsuccessful." Is it possible that the strict suppression of warmth and emotion in a previous lifetime may have carried over into this one?

Dr. Smith's host, Dr. Kelsey, is a British psychiatrist, and his wife, Joan Grant, is the well-known psychic and author of such outstanding books on reincarnation as *Winged Pharaoh* and *Far Memories*. During Dr. Smith's visit with them in France, another of their house guests netted a magnificent stag beetle, and Dr. Smith eagerly laid claim to it. While in high school he had collected beetles, but only once had snared a stag, and the memory of it still made him uncomfortable; for although he thought that he had killed it in a merciful manner, before mounting it, the beetle revived and had to undergo a second "death."

To clear his thoughts of the beetle, Dr. Smith took a motorbike ride in the countryside surrounding the Kelseys' property; and on his return, their dogs greeted him with such unconcealed affection that others remarked on his way with animals. Joan Grant Kelsey was also impatiently awaiting him. She said that while preparing dinner, she had beheld a vision of "the figure of Christ surrounded by discarnates" and heard the words, "He that is cruel to his fellow man cuts himself off from his neighbors, but he who is cruel to an animal cuts himself off from the gods." Joan said she had sensed that the message was intended for Dr. Smith, although she could not understand why; nor could he, because he is extremely fond of animals.

He says that after retiring that night, while in a state of semisleep he suddenly experienced "a vivid impression of myself castrating Christ." The shock of the vision was so overpowering that he tossed in his bed the remainder of the night, unable to sleep. The next morning, when he joined the Kelseys for breakfast, Joan exclaimed that she had been "shown" Dr. Smith's most recent incarnation during the night. She said that he had been a laboratory assistant to Serge Voronoff, the famed Russian scientist whose work in transplanting monkey glands to humans for sexual rejuvenation had electrified the Western world, earlier in this century. Dr. Smith's principal task in that lifetime, she continued, had been the removal of testicles from monkeys, sometimes without proper anesthesia, and that in approximately 1923, while in his early thirties, he died from a monkey bite on one of his forearms.

"It was my right arm!" Dr. Smith exclaimed, grabbing himself just below the elbow; for as Joan described the incident, a flash of memory seemed to tell him the exact location of the fatal bite. If her vision was correct, only four years had elapsed between the death of the research assistant and his rebirth in Chicago as the son of a doctor. If true, it could also have had a profound effect on this lifetime; for during his internship Dr. Smith exhibited considerable surgical skill, but so hated the idea of cutting and hurting that he became a psychiatrist instead of a surgeon.

Dr. Smith had told no one of his unsettling vision of the "castration of Christ," but after Joan Grant seemingly awakened a past-life memory of the monkey bite, he felt that he had a clue to its significance, for Christ taught that "Whatsoever ye do unto the least of these, my brethren, ye do it also unto me." With profound thanksgiving that he had not yet killed and mounted the newly found stag beetle, Dr. Smith hastened to his room and set it free.

To understand others, we must first understand ourselves, and because Dr. Smith courageously met himself head-on, he is unquestionably a more capable psychiatrist.

Dr. Stanley Krippner, director of the famed dream laboratory at Maimonides Medical Center in New York, says that his only personal experience with possible recall of earlier lives occurred while in a psychedelic state, under legal test conditions. He said that during that period he felt "as if I could travel in the past, present, or future." Describing the sensation, he continued:

"At one moment, I was in the court of Kublai Khan, admiring the rich brocades of the emperor's gown and noting the fine, detailed embroidery of his courtiers' cloaks. Within an instant I was at the court of Versailles with Benjamin Franklin. The great old sage was more impressive in his wisdom than were the king and queen in their crowns and furs. The scene shifted to the New World, where Thomas Jefferson was explaining his latest invention at Monticello, and then to the nation's capital, where the tragic profile of Lincoln presented itself. Lincoln's features faded, and those of Kennedy appeared. My eyes opened, and they were filled with tears." This sequence of mind pictures appeared, incidentally, eighteen months before John F. Kennedy—like Lincoln—was assassinated in office.

In another session with LSD, Dr. Krippner found himself seemingly in Hawaii, with a young lady saying to him, "You are no longer a malihini [newcomer] but a kamaaina [old-timer]." Next he saw an Arabian village "so delicately poised that I hesitated to breathe for fear of destroying" the images. "I could see the towers, the turrets, the mosque, and the minarets." In subsequent sequences he saw himself as a Spanish bullfighter, as a high priest of the Aztecs, as a sea captain, and as a drunken soldier at Calvary. Dr. Krippner has no idea whether he could have been viewing brief glimpses of his own past, or whether the images stemmed from his reading or imagination. All who dip into the fascinating realm of reincarnation agree, however, that we have only begun to scratch the surface of the mysteries surrounding man and his inner self.

The Reverend George F. Emery, pastor of the First Methodist Church in Lacon, Illinois, made his first preaching mission to the Middle East in 1966, and after delivering a sermon in Cairo, Egypt, he accompanied a group of other pastors and friends to the nearby pyramids at Giza. The youthful minister is an athletic type, full of vigor and vitality, and the moment that he glimpsed the Great Pyramid he announced that he intended to scale it. Some of his colleagues volunteered to join him and he was in the forefront as they eagerly began the climb, but he had advanced no more than a few feet when he was "overcome by a terrific sense of gloom and fear."

"I was dumbfounded at my reaction," he confesses, "but I knew that I couldn't go on. The others kept shouting at me to keep climbing, but I carefully inched my way backward, until

I could sit down at the base of the pyramid and close my eyes. Immediately, I saw slaves pushing the heavy blocks into place, and amid the bustle of the colorful mental image I clearly identified myself with one of the young workmen. I was laboriously helping to push a heavy block of stone into place, when I heard a piercing shriek, and saw the blocks collapsing on me. I knew that I had died as a slave in Egypt, while helping to erect that pyramid."

The Rev. Mr. Emery found the experience extremely disquieting, because he had until recently scoffed at the idea of reincarnation. He consequently made no mention of the eerie drama that had unfolded before his inner eye, and proceeded on to the Holy Land, the next stop on his itinerary. A few days later, while occupying the rear seat of an Israeli bus en route from Jerusalem to Lake Tiberius, he momentarily closed his eyes for relaxation, and inwardly saw a camel caravan passing along the same route. "Litter-bearers were carrying their masters on elaborate chairs," he says of the vision, "and I myself, feeling very princely in my silken robes, was being borne on one of the litters. The impression was so overpowering that I was lost in the mood of another moment in time. Therefore, I was physically shocked when the loudspeaker began to crackle, and the Israeli guide announced, "This is the route that in former times was used by Persian princes on their way to Tiberius for winter vacations. They were carried by litter-bearers."

The bus continued through the green hills and valleys of Israel until it reached the Sea of Galilee, or Tiberius, as it is called today. Then the road followed the curving sweep of the sea, and as the bus halted at a barren spot along the shore, the Rev. Mr. Emery says that he had a sudden compulsion to leap out, press his face to the earth and kiss the ground.

"This was home to me," he says simply. "I didn't know where we were, but I knew that I had spent the happiest days of my life there. Closing my eyes, I saw a group of people in loose robes, their faces aglow, grouped around a man whose back was turned to me. I seemed to be a lad in my late teens, and as I stood about fifty feet from the assemblage, watching intently, a woman with beautiful eyes and dark-brown hair came over to me, took me by the hand and said, 'Come, I want you to meet the Master.' At that moment the guide turned on the loudspeaker of the bus, and announced, 'This is the ruins of Magdala, home of Mary Magdalene.' That really shook me, because all my life I have associated myself more closely with Mary Magdalene than any other Biblical figure, feeling great empathy and compassion for her. To me, this seemed another authentic memory of a past life—an experience with such dramatic impact that even today I find myself longing to return to Magdala."

On his return to America, the pastor was still reluctant to speak of these strange occurrences to anyone, but they stirred his curiosity about an earlier happening that he had virtually ignored. The year before his trip to the Middle East, he had been told by a psychic that if it was "meant" for a person to become aware of previous incarnations, the knowledge would be made known to him in meditation. The next morning he decided to put it to the test, and as he prepared to begin his regular period of meditation, he asked, "Is it important for me to know my identity in a past life?" He says that the answer came in the affirmative, and when he requested that the information be supplied, he clearly heard the words, "You were George Whitfield."

The inner voice continued after a moment, saying that he needed to use the knowledge of his many struggles in that life, but in a different kind of spiritual revolution; not as a mass evangelist, but in small group ministry. "There are many lessons to learn that you did not learn before," he was told. "That is why you have turned down so many chances to become an evangelist in this lifetime."

The Rev. Mr. Emery says that he was flabbergasted by the message, and puzzled by its source. Was his imagination running away with him, or had he actually heard these words? The thought had certainly never entered his conscious mind, for he had firmly considered himself "a Wesley man."

"I didn't like Whitfield's Calvanistic bent any more than John Wesley had," he says thoughtfully. "In fact, about all I knew of George Whitfield was that he had helped Wesley found the Methodist Church, that he was an eloquent preacher and great witness, but because of his Calvinistic leanings had broken with Wesley. I didn't even like his name, George, which was also my own, so I put the matter on the shelf. It was something that I didn't want to think about."

After his soul-stirring experiences in the Middle East, the pastor decided that perhaps he should know more about George Whitfield. In reading biographies of him, he was surprised to learn that the eighteenth-century English evangelist was buried at Newburyport, Massachusetts. This was only eighteen miles from Portsmouth, New Hampshire, where George Emery was born; and he had always felt a strange kinship with Newburyport, because although there were larger and nearer places where his family could have shopped, they had invariably gone to Newburyport during his boyhood.

Whitfield had been a priest of the Church of England, and "confidant of outcasts," preaching in shipyards, foundries, churches and fields. He had been called both devil and saint as he rose from obscurity to international prominence, galvanizing the sinners of two continents to repent, and he made fourteen evangelistic trips to America to conduct revivals.

The Rev. Mr. Emery was surprised to read that in the fall of 1770, twenty-four hours before his death, George Whitfield had preached his last sermon in Portsmouth. One hundred and sixty years later, George Emery was born in Portsmouth. They even had the same birth sign, Sagittarius, and an astrological chart which had once been drawn for Emery could have equally described the great English evangelist.

Almost from the time that George Emery learned to talk, he was possessed with evangelistic zeal, and after preaching his first sermon at the age of sixteen, numerous members of the audience said that he could be "another Billy Sunday." While in high school and college, admirers urged him to give up the thought of going to theological seminary and become an evangelist instead, but he resisted the temptation; and throughout his years at State Teachers College in Farmington, Maine, and the Boston University School of Theology he held the pastorate at a church with more than six hundred members.

He was already making such a name for himself as a stirring speaker that, upon his graduation, friends and instructors were stunned when he turned down an offer to become the pastor of a congregation where his eloquent voice would be raised every Sunday. Instead, he chose to go into small group and spiritual healing ministry at the First Methodist Church in Springfield, Illinois, where he would be preaching no oftener than three or four times a year. Thinking back on that decision today, the Rev. Mr. Emery believes that he unconsciously refrained from following the evangelistic course of Whitfield, in order to learn new lessons and meet the chal-

lenges of a different type of spiritual revolution in this lifetime.

Now a firm believer in reincarnation, the pastor drove to
Newburyport in the summer of 1967, after attending the
Methodist Conference in the East. George Whitfield was buried at the Old South Presbyterian Church, and after the rector had shown the Reverend and Mrs. Emery about the
premises, he took them downstairs to the crypt below the pul-
pit. Had the rector been aware of the psychical experience
which seemed to link his visitor with the celebrated man
whose body reposed in the crypt, that would doubtless have
been the extent of the tour.

As it was, the good rector unlocked the door of the tomb.
There, staring sightlessly out at the minister from Illinois was
a replica of Whitfield's skull. It is doubtful whether many
others who "identify" with a person now dead can match this
eerie experience.

III

The Past Is Prologue

AN eminent woman scientist whose name is familiar to most adult Americans became interested in reincarnation three decades ago, through her involvement with a twelve-year-old boy who could speak fluent German and Persian while in spontaneous trance. Neither he nor his parents consciously knew any language other than English, but scholars who studied the youngster declared that his German was that spoken in the early sixteenth century, and his Persian predated the German by two centuries.

In his waking state, the boy's principal interests were baseball and fishing. He was a mediocre student, disinclined to study, but when in trance he spoke with erudition on a vast range of knowledge including medicine, religion and philosophy. He continued to puzzle investigators until, on reaching maturity, he lost his power to go into trance and became a "normal" adult, with a wife and children.

The case triggered a lasting interest in reincarnation for the woman scientist, whom I shall call Jane Winthrop, to respect her wish for privacy. Intrigued by the possibility that anyone under properly induced hypnosis might be able to recall previous lifetimes, she invited a group of volunteers to participate in a series of experiments at her home in Los Angeles. Major Arthur Knight, a psychologist who has done considerable work in hypnotic regression, conducted the sessions, and told the group that while stationed with the U.S. Air Force in England during World War II, he sometimes gave exhausted fliers a "three weeks' vacation," in whatever place they most wished to be, by putting them into trance. Within an hour they awakened refreshed, as if they had actually relaxed at the seashore or mountains, ready for their next flight.

Major Knight instructed Jane Winthrop's friends to close their eyes and imagine themselves lying on a green lawn, or floating on water, while the tension gradually left their feet and ankles, knees and thighs, abdomen, back, chest and neck, the eyes, ears, mouth and scalp. "Your mind can hold only one thought at a time," he explained, "so those of you who wish to be hypnotic subjects may imagine that your eyes are so tightly closed that they cannot be opened. If you keep that thought uppermost, when you try to open them they will only become more tightly closed." Many of them in the room passed this simple test. Next he put them into deeper trance by suggesting that they clasp their fingers together, pushing palm against palm while thinking that they could not be pulled apart. The third test was to hold out the left arm and tell oneself that it was a bar of steel, too rigid to be bent. Anyone who can pass this test, he said, can have surgery under hypnosis without an anesthetic.

Unlike a stage hypnotist, who thinks that it makes a better show to render his subject's mind unconscious, Major Knight stressed to each volunteer that his mind would remain keen and alert throughout the demonstration, and that he would afterward recall everything that he had said. Then he began a countdown, to regress the group to some childhood experience, when suddenly the executive of an aircraft factory broke into uncontrollable sobbing. Soothingly asked the trouble, he blubbered: "I'm nine years old. My father and mother are getting a divorce, and Father is going away. I'll never see him again."

After the executive was brought out of trance, Major Knight turned his attention to a heavyset, Middle-Western woman of Protestant faith, regressing her to several childhood memories, before saying, "Now it's a few days before your birth." Instantly she drew herself into a uterine position, as he continued: "While I count to twenty, you will go back before conception. Back . . . back . . . back. When I stop counting, you can tell us if there is anything you feel or hear. You will speak only English. Your mind will be unusually alert." The countdown began, and as he reached twenty her face assumed a mature, peaceful, almost saintly mien. She began to answer his questions in a mellow voice totally unlike her normal Midwestern twang, and although she was ordinarily a rather awkward woman, her gestures now were exceedingly graceful. Identifying herself as a nun in Asia Minor during the third century A.D., she said that her duty was caring for orphaned children in a Catholic school. As she described her flowing black habit, she repeatedly bowed her head as if in prayer.

Asked to describe her death, she said that fighting raged nearby, and that as she and the children fled up a steep mountain pass, huge rocks fell and crushed her. "The soldiers are waving the white flag of truce," she continued softly, and then made long, sweeping gestures in opposite directions. The hypnotist asked what she was doing, and she replied, "The soldiers are covering my body with a white cloth." As the psychologist slowly brought her from under hypnosis, she resumed her normally choppy gestures, but all in the room felt that for a few minutes they had been privileged to know a selfless woman of true nobility, who had found serenity in life and death.

The next subject was Alice, a slight, middle-aged woman whose voice became so soft that the group strained to hear as she said, "I'm riding horseback on my father's estate in France." Her body suddenly lurched, her leg pulled behind her, and between sobs she gasped that she had been thrown by the horse, which was now dragging her. The writhings of her body and her terrified expression convinced those present that the agony was excruciatingly real, and Major Knight quickly brought her back to consciousness, after telling her that she would no longer feel any pain.

The psychologist's practiced eye had meanwhile spotted an excellent male subject, a slender young doctor with blond hair, ruddy complexion and clean-cut good looks. The physician obligingly stretched out on the sofa, and after being regressed beyond his present life, he announced that he was twenty years old. He said that his low shoes had large silver buckles, and that he was also wearing white knee stockings, tight blue silk pants, and a shirt with white ruffles at the throat and wrists. Those who knew him commented in whispers on the marked change of personality as he spelled out his name, Norman Devereau.

Responding to questioning, he said, "I'm in a castle. It's built of stone. The ceilings are arched. They're very high. Up near the ceiling is a stained-glass window with sunshine pouring through it."

"What country are you in?" the hypnotist asked.

"France."

"Do you live near a city?"

"We don't go to cities much. Once I went to Cologne."

Asked to describe the happiest time of that life, he told of a salon to which guests had come to hear him play the harpsichord. Although more animated than usual, he coughed repeatedly; and when asked if he was well, he replied, "No, I spit up blood all the time."

"What would that disease be called now?"

"Consumption."

"Let's go ahead again. Describe your death for us."

"I've been sick for many years. I want to die."

"How old are you?"

"Thirty-four."

"Aren't your parents or wife with you?"

"No, I never married. No one is with me but an old servant. She's a sort of nurse."

On being told that the spirit had now left the body, the subject heaved a great sigh of relief, and a look of peace settled on his face. Told to describe his burial, he spoke in an odd monotone, saying, "Servants come in the dead of night and break through the wall into the room where my body is lying. They are slipping the body through the hole, and are carrying it a long way up the mountain. Now they are dropping it into a steep ravine and covering it with rocks." He said that no marker had been placed on his burial site, and on being asked why his body was treated so unceremoniously, he responded, "Because the peasants are terribly afraid of the disease. Everyone is! Only my most faithful servants would come near me."

"What is the year of your death?"

"Fifteen hundred and forty-seven."

Major Knight, turning to others in the room, briefly outlined his understanding of karma, and said that if possible he would like to find out why the man had been forced to suffer so greatly in that life. Turning back to the subject, he said,

"Now, I want to regress you still further in time. Tell us why, in this life you have just described, you never married, had few friends, had to suffer and die early, and even to be denied a decent burial." He then began another countdown, while the young doctor lay inert. At the count of twenty, a look of suffering twisted his features, and as his face contorted with pain, his breathing became more labored. Again and again the hypnotist prodded him with questions but the doctor merely stammered until, after what appeared to be great inner turmoil, he finally blurted, "I stoned a woman to death." Again the psychologist addressed the group and commented: "Every time a person describes a life of suffering, he will invariably tell us that he has made someone else suffer in a previous life. It should make us pause and think before we act."

After the handsome young physician was brought out of trance, guests excitedly questioned Major Knight, who said that he began his work with prebirth regression through sheer chance. In 1930, while working on his master's degree in psychology at the University of Minnesota, some of the students volunteered as guinea pigs to provide material for his thesis on hypnosis. On one occasion, while regressing a student to age four, another caller burst into the room and so distracted him that he automatically continued counting. When he finally stopped and asked the subject his name, the young man gave a different one from his own, and assumed another personality while describing a life totally unlike his present one.

Some of the volunteers, that first evening at Jane Winthrop's home, described such charming birth scenes that at a subsequent session the woman scientist remarked that she would like to relive her own birth under hypnosis. Major Knight thereupon regressed her "to zero," after telling her that she would afterward recall every detail, and this is her own account of what transpired:

"I had no sooner curled up in blissful intrauterine comfort than my body appeared to become a battering ram. The back of my head was repeatedly hit against the curved surface of the pelvic bone, causing an agonizing headache which persisted until I was rehypnotized several hours later, to remove the pain. Next I felt that I was being squeezed to death, and then I was dangling in midair, held only by my head while my feet were still in the vaginal canal, so terrified of falling that the fear itself became excruciating. Simultaneously, I felt as if I were in an arctic blizzard, which must have been caused by rapid evaporation of moisture through the change from internal body to room temperature. Piercing pains kept shooting through my eyes, and when Art Knight asked me to repeat the first words I had heard spoken, I replied in a disconsolate tone, 'It's another girl.' The words made me feel so unwelcome that I wanted to cry forever."

Jane's parents and the doctor who delivered her are no longer living, so she is unable to check the validity of this "memory," but she does know that her mother died shortly after giving birth to her. Major Knight next regressed Jane beyond birth, and as he finished counting, she says that she beheld a vivid scene which seemed as familiar as her own living room today.

"The friends around me had ceased to exist, as had the room itself," she recalls, "yet I felt as completely myself as one does in ordinary life. I was merely another self, and the time almost seemed like 'now.' I was sitting on a huge boulder, dangling my bare feet toward a gushing torrent which was confined by immense gray boulders. To my right was a delightful waterfall some ten feet high, and so near that I could feel the spray on my face. Perhaps fifty feet in front of me were many tall trees, and beyond them the woods thickened into a dense forest. Directly behind me, a well-worn path led through a sunlit plot of shaggy grass to a small, thatch-roofed cottage, which was completely surrounded by a forest so dense that no wisp of sunlight penetrated to the brown earth. I had never seen such a thick, dark forest, nor such stately trees, whose lowest branches were at least twenty feet from the ground, but several years later when visiting Brussels for the first time, I felt that the King's Forest at the edge of that city was almost identical to that which I had seen under hypnosis. I wanted Art to ask me about the cottage, but he kept asking my age, sex, and what I looked like. For the first time I became aware of my appearance, which was anything but glamorous. I somehow knew that I was a man about twenty, that my homespun red shirt was open at the neck, and my skin-tight blue trousers were frayed at the knees. I knew that I had pale blue eyes with blond lashes, a homely face, and a startling shock of shoulder-length, carrot-red hair which appeared never to have been washed, combed or cut. It would be difficult to imagine a more uncouth country bumpkin."

Finally permitted to describe the cottage, Jane did so in minute detail, telling of the hand-hewn boards, the peg-legged stools, the location of rooms, the fire pits and iron cooking pots. "It seemed that I was an only child, and that my parents and I had lived all our lives in this tiny cottage," she muses. "I had married early, but both my wife and mother were now dead. I owned a large herd of sheep and a few cattle, and since the latter were in scarce supply, I felt that owning them placed me in a higher social bracket by neighborhood standards.

"It is a weird experience to hear yourself talking with an unfamiliar voice, and to have words pour out with a total absence of forethought or preknowledge of what is about to be said. Each bit of information comes as a surprise, making it seem as if you are listening to someone else speak. When Art asked me in what country I was living, I replied that it was Holland, and when he took me farther ahead in that lifetime, to the age of forty-eight, I announced that I now had a buxom young wife of twenty-six who was good-natured, had bright blue eyes, apple-red cheeks and a scrubbed, starched look. Her hair, which she wore in two thick braids, was the color of fresh straw, and I was hopelessly in love with her. Our cottage was much larger than the earlier one, and scrupulously clean, with a fireplace against one wall and an extremely high double bed on the opposite wall."

Major Knight instructed Jane to move ahead in time to the year of death, and she instantly "knew" that she was sexually impotent. Sounding deeply depressed, she muttered, "I feel old, old, old. But I'm very prosperous, have lots of sheep and cattle, and my young wife's still adorable." She gave her age as "fifty-six, I think," and then was asked to describe her death. Jane says that as hazy pictures gradually clarified she saw two oddly dressed peasants engaged in a fistfight. One of them, whom she suddenly recognized as herself, fell to the ground and was carried by two men through the woods and into the cottage. "Then I both saw and felt myself lying in the high bed," she recalls, "while my wife moved rapidly about, her wooden shoes clumping on the bare floor. Every cell in my body ached and a cruel pain stabbed at my throat. My breathing became loud and labored, and a knife wound in my throat seemed to be bleeding profusely."

Major Knight told Jane that the spirit had now left the body, and asked her what she could see. "I seem to be floating in the corner of the room above the bed," she replied. "I'm terribly glad to be dead. I can look down and see my body. It seemed little and shriveled. The knees are flexed and the head is turned to one side." Asked to describe the burial, she said that she hovered above two men in a forest, watching them make a coffin of rough boards, irregularly cut. "The men carried the coffin near the cottage, and into it they unceremoniously dumped my body, still clothed as before, the knees still flexed and the head turned to one side. They've laid two rough boards across the top, and are using small knives to gouge holes for wooden pegs, which they are driving in with large mallets."

The hypnotist asked her to move a little ahead in time, and see whether there was a marker for the grave. She replied that they placed a small cross, made of dark split wood, at one end, and the date, 1463. Then, in an anguished voice, she added, "Nobody cried when I died. Not a single person cried!"

Before bringing her out of trance, Major Knight told her that she would feel wonderfully rested and alert, and she did; but during the remainder of the evening, her mind seethed with questions. Where, she asked herself, could such a yarn have come from? Was it pure imagination, or something that she had read and forgotten? But how could either explanation account for the violent emotions that she had felt: the worshipful adoration of the young wife, the sense of shame about her sexual impotency, the actual pain while dying, and the tremendous relief which came with death?

So many questions continued to puzzle her that, several years later, Jane asked to be hypnotized again. She had thought that she might describe a different lifetime, but as the count concluded she knew that her bright red hair was as uncombed as before. This time she was leaning against the cottage, so that she viewed the waterfall and forest from a different angle, and when directed to go backward in time to the age of ten, she declared that her father was a gamekeeper on a large estate, but was allowed to keep his own sheep. Jane gave her name as Hans Deverter, said that their food staples were deer, quail, wild duck, mutton and bread, and described her mother as a fat woman who was leaning over a firepit to bake rye bread. She watched her bury oblong, somewhat flattened loaves on a thick layer of ashes which covered hot rocks, and somehow knew that the ashes would be easily brushed from the brown crust when the bread was baked.

Taken forward in time, she told of trips to fairs with the sheep, and after again describing her death, she said of it: "During life your body always seems to be in the way, but now I feel light. I'm floating and drifting through the air. It feels wonderful. There doesn't seem to be nights anymore. I'm floating over the meadow where my sheep used to graze. My wife is so alone there in the woods that I don't want to leave her." Major Knight moved her still farther ahead, and she immediately noticed how much her buxom young wife had aged. "She isn't fat anymore. She's tall and angular. Her hair's stringy now, as if she didn't care about fixing it. I don't think she's very well." After another lapse of time she described her wife's death, and said that after neighbors lowered her body into the grave, all of them cried. Sadness overcame her at this point, and she groaned, "Nobody cried when I died."

Some who scoff at the theory of reincarnation argue that a hypnotized subject is simply trying to glamorize himself or please the hypnotist, but the cases which have come to my attention fail to fit into this category. Most of the lifetimes described are drab and ordinary, some even shameful. Surely the average person, if giving free rein to imagination, would assign himself more dramatic or heroic roles in ages past.

For instance, during another experiment a pretty, slender blonde from New York "saw" herself standing on a bridge spanning the Thames in London. Under questioning her story gradually unfolded: "I'm a woman. I guess I'm fifty-four. I'm real short. I'm terribly fat. I can see great rolls of fat on my arms." She stroked her upper arm and seemingly smoothed a huge protruding stomach. Suddenly she uttered a series of piercing screams that must have alarmed the Winthrops' neighbors, and when Major Knight attempted to question her, she sobbed: "I'm afraid . . . I'm afraid. I've stolen something . . . a bag of something. I'm afraid! I'm hiding in a doorway, crouched down in a corner. There's cobblestones on the street. A soldier's coming. I don't know if he sees me." Stark terror stood in her eyes as she gasped, "I . . . don't . . . know." Her voice died away, and after a long pause she murmured incredulously, "They've hung me!"

Major Knight asked what happened to the body after the

spirit left it, and when the woman spoke again, her voice was sweet and low. "It just hangs there," she mused, "as a warning for others not to steal." Under continued prodding, she said, "There's a man in a black cape. He's going to take it down. He comes up some steps to get my body." Then, with great forcefulness, she added, "I'm not that body. I don't care what happens to that body. I don't care." She placed the year as 1737, and after being regressed to an earlier lifetime to determine why she had met such a tragic demise, she said belligerently, "A little boy. I pushed him in the river. Men are rowing out to him in a boat, but he's already drowned." Asked why she did such a thing, she muttered in a hard, bitter voice, "Because he wasn't mine. I couldn't have any."

The psychologist, turning to the group, remarked, "It happens again and again in prebirth regressions. If a person meets a violent death, he has nearly always taken another's life in a previous incarnation. It occurs so often that I've learned to look for it. Almost literally it seems to be proving the Biblical injunction, 'As a man sows, so shall he also reap.' "

The next subject was a university student with a high-pitched voice, who was given to frequent giggling spells. When regressed to her sixth birthday in this lifetime she talked with a thick Brooklyn accent, whined about her "runny" nose, said that none of the other children liked her, and complained that she had received only "crummy" presents for Christmas, but upon being taken "back back back to a previous lifetime," her voice assumed the ladylike quality of a highly cultured person. She found herself in a garden, watching cherry blossoms by moonlight, and listening to the tinkle of a brook. She said that she was wearing a white kimono embroidered with pink rosebuds, wore "tabi" on her feet, and had glossy black hair.

"I'm sad, sad," she sighed. "I want to write, but I'm only allowed to paint, and arrange flowers. I'm nothing but a woman." She spelled her name Yumiko Ichikawa, pronouncing it You-mee-ko Cheeka-wa, and continued, "I'm betrothed. My parents have arranged it, and I'm not supposed to see him, but I peeked. He's the same age I am, with black hair and fine features. He's his father's wonder."

Major Knight asked what the young man did for a living, and she replied, "He doesn't have to do anything. His father is a wealthy samurai. My father is a high government official. He isn't home much, because he has a geisha."

Asked if she ever traveled, she said that she had gone by boat through the islands with her mother, and that "we also have rickshaws, and an aka pulls them." Since the word "aka" was unfamiliar to anyone in the room, the hypnotist said he assumed that the carts were pulled by people. Generations of disdain edged her voice as she loftily replied, "You might call them that."

In answer to other questions she said that her parents were Buddhists, but that she believed only in "the stars and the sea." Moved ahead in time, she said that she did not like being married. "My husband doesn't like me much. We are not friendly. He will take a geisha one of these days. I don't want children. They'll be as unhappy as I am, but I'm going to have a baby."

Major Knight again took her forward and asked whether the baby was a boy or a girl. A warm sweetness replaced the crisp, Japanese-accented voice as she said, "I don't know. I died. The baby also died. A woman is there, but she has put a cloth around the baby. I can't see." Queried about her own body, she replied, "They put a beautiful white kimono on it. It lies in a casket. My husband is there, but he doesn't care. They bury the body in the garden, so it can go to its ancestors. There's no marker, but a record is added at the family altar." She said that death occurred in her twenty-sixth year, in 1848; and when asked why she came back in her present body, she exclaimed, "Now I'm an American, I can do things."

After being brought from under hypnosis, the student was astonished at the story she had told. As is often the case, she said that she has always been fascinated by the idea of Japan, although she has never been there or known Japanese people. Similarly, the woman who described her death as a nun said that she has been so intrigued by Catholic sisters that she often stops to watch them on the street. The skeptic could argue that this interest causes subjects to dramatize themselves in such a role while under hypnosis, whereas the believer feels that a previous incarnation explains the present fascination with the subject.

Debbie White, a slim, auburn-haired woman with a distinctive Virginia drawl, proved to be a particularly apt subject. In one of our sessions with Major Knight, she told us of a life in early India, when her traveling companions were killed by bandits who left her to die, without food or water. She vividly described crawling over the hot sand, desperately searching for grains of spilled rice, "until the sun finally got me." Another time she spoke of a life in Persia, where her husband rented camels for caravans, but in a third session the count had barely concluded before she spoke in a decidedly French accent, saying, "There's our house on the hill. It's very large, and built of stone. The tall, narrow windows look like slits. It belonged to my father's father, and to his father for hundreds of years back. Their pictures all hang in the great hall. Oh, we're not titled, but we're prominent. My father's a general in Napoleon's army."

Asked her name, she spelled out, "Blanche Barpour," pronouncing it Blahnssh Baapour. "My mother died when I was born," she told us. "I live alone with my father, and we have lots of servants. Father's hair is red, and when he gets angry it stands straight up. He wears a pointed beard, small but distinguished. He's handsome, but his face is red, especially when he's angry. Then he's like a thundercloud. The Barpours all have violent tempers. He could get married, but he won't. He has lots of women. I'm very willful. I boss him, and he lets me get away with it."

Told to locate the Barpour estate, she continued, "We live a half day's ride from Marseilles. My father and I go there in the coach-and-four to the opera. Guards have to ride with us, or highwaymen would attack along the road." Wistfulness crept into her voice as she remarked, "I've never actually been to the Mediterranean. I'd like to, but Father says we can't go near the water because of the rats. We seldom stay in town because of the rats. They're big . . . and everywhere. The streets are so narrow, and the cobblestones so filthy! Everything's dirty. The city smells. It's full of ragged children, and people throw awful things out of the windows." Under continued questioning, she said that she loved horses, and her favorite was Mimi, a mare her father gave her as a peace offering when she was seventeen.

Regressed to that age to learn more about the peace offering, Debbie said, "I'm hiding in the stables watching the men breed a mare. No one knows I'm here. I shouldn't be here, but I'm curious. Someday I may want to breed horses, and I want to know these things. If I'm old enough to get married, why am I too young to see a mare bred?" Moved forward again, she recalled with an airy laugh, "That's when father found me, and we quarreled. He shouted at me saying ladies don't go to the stables, and I shouted right back. Father never apologizes. The mare that he gave me is as close as he ever came to an apology."

She said that she was engaged to Charles Chevez, a lieutenant under her father's command, and that he and her father both wore the same uniforms: tricornered hats and blue coats with double straps across their chests.

After Major Knight moved her ahead a few years, she complained, "I'm not happy. My husband's all right, I suppose, but he doesn't know how to handle me. He's afraid of me. He's a captain in the army now, and away most of the time. We have a little girl, Barbara, who looks like him. Pierre's four now. He has red hair like my father. I was very sick when he was born. I didn't want him, and somehow he knew it. He can't forgive me." The psychologist counted seven, to take her that many years forward, and asked if her husband and father were there.

"No, they went to the Ukraine," she sighed. Apparently referring to Napoleon's disastrous invasion of Russia, she continued, "It was winter, and snowing all the time. My father was killed in action, but Charles died with measles." She rolled the latter word disdainfully off her tongue, as if she considered it a less than heroic way for a soldier to die. Asked to describe the last day of her own life, she murmured, "I'm thirty-seven. I'm tired. Not sick, just tired. Bruce sent me a message and I came here to Marseilles, but I shouldn't be here."

"Who's Bruce?"

"A British soldier, a captain. His britches are white and his jacket is deep red, with brass buttons. I'm in love with him."

"What are you doing?"

"I'm in this bedroom with Bruce. Oh, I shouldn't be here! Some French soldiers break in and are taking us away. The people are rioting in the streets. They're hungry. So much noise! Yelling and shouting, yelling and shouting. They're bursting into wealthy people's homes and killing them, they're so hungry and angry."

"Are you arrested because you're with Bruce?"

"That's right. They don't know who I am. They don't know that my father was a French general, and I won't tell them. They're putting us into a two-wheeled cart with fifteen or sixteen other people. They're pushing me so hard against the railing that it hurts my stomach. I can't breathe, there are so many of us. Oh, it hurts! Bruce is behind me, but he can't help."

By now she was sobbing, and tears flowed down her cheeks. "They've taken us to an open place . . . a town square. There are buildings all around, and a sort of scaffolding in the center. Oh, it's a guillotine," she screamed, using the French pronunciation. "I'm so frightened, so frightened. We have to walk up thirteen steps. Thirteen. Thirteen. They're going to behead everyone in the cart. They make me watch it. Bruce says he's sorry, and 'easy does it.' Bruce is killed before I am, *ohhhhhhhhh!*"

Major Knight broke into her prolonged sobbing to assure her that she would feel no pain. Thus reassured, she continued, "They tied my hands behind my back. I keep stumbling over my skirt as I climb the steps, and think of my children. They need their mother! But Bruce is gone now, so I don't care. I loved him! I loved him!"

The hypnotist soothingly reiterated that she would not suffer, and she said, "They make me kneel down. There's a hollowed-out place my head fits into. Something else fits over the back of my neck so I can't move. My head's turned to the right."

Those of us in the room were rigid with horror. Our knuckles showed white as we gripped the arms of our chairs, and after a prolonged silence, Debbie's voice continued, "The blade falls, but it kind of bounces. There's a nick in it. So many heads have been falling, it doesn't quite do it. Blood is gushing over my shoulder. I can't breathe! I'm choking and gurgling . . . choking and gurgling. At last they drop the blade again." The gasping and sobbing abruptly stopped, and after a few moments she spoke softly, saying, "I feel so relieved. My head is lying in a big wicker basket with several others. The bodies are being taken away to be burned."

"Did you find Bruce again?" Art asked.

"Yes, immediately," she sighed happily. "But I keep getting farther and farther away. Farther away . . ." Her voice trailed off into silence.

IV

Nothing Is Forgotten

HYPNOTISM is as old as recorded history, having been known to ancient Persians, Egyptians and Greeks, but scientific interest in the subject dates from the late eighteenth century when Franz Mesmer, a Viennese physician, used it in the treatment of patients. It soon became discredited, but some doctors retained an interest in "Mesmerism," and in the mid-nineteenth century the English physician, James Braid, coined the words hypnotism and hypnosis. Thereafter, scientifically trained men began serious study of the subject, and in the decade of the 1950's both the British and American medical associations formally approved its medical use.

Many dentists now employ hypnosis to numb pain during tooth extraction, psychiatrists use it in the treatment of disturbed patients, and physicians have induced a trance state to alleviate discomfort during surgery and childbirth. Hypnotism is also used by our military intelligence services, inasmuch as agents who are hypnotized after their return from spy missions can produce total recall of all that they have seen, even to the number of slats in a Venetian blind above a desk that they have ransacked; and the Soviets are reportedly sponsoring a crash program in hypnosis and extrasensory perception.

The Encyclopedia Britannica, in a chapter on hypnosis, declares: "The [hypnotized] subject is not, as is commonly and

46

wrongly believed, without will power, or under the power of the hypnotist. Instead, the relationship between the subject and the hypnotist is one of inter-personal cooperation based upon mutually acceptable and reasonable considerations. Hence, the subject cannot be forced to do things against his will, as is sometimes claimed." Of regression in age under hypnosis, it says: "The subject experiences a retrogressive loss of memories, learnings and responses, and those belonging to an earlier age are re-established."

Hypnosis can be extremely dangerous if used by an untrained person, or by one unversed in psychology. An emotionally unstable girl who served as a subject for an amateur hypnotist relived such traumatic childhood experiences that she became mentally ill, and had to be confined to an institution. Another woman attempted suicide after reexperiencing a rape at the age of four, an event that until then had mercifully been blocked from her consciousness. Hypnotism is not a toy to be used for idle amusement, but in the proper hands it has performed enormous good, freeing terminal cancer patients from agonizing pain, relieving suffering in severe burns, and rendering bearable the torture of drug withdrawal from dope addicts.

Dr. James L. Rowland, a prominent Midwestern physician, has told us of the case of an athletic teen-aged girl who, while competing in a diving contest, suddenly "froze" on the diving board. She did not know why, but she was thereafter so terrified of the water that her parents took her to Dr. Rowland for treatment of her hysteria. Under hypnosis, she recalled that she had seen a moving shadow in the water just as she was preparing to dive, but when the physician could find no explanation for her unusual reaction to a shadow, in this lifetime, he secured permission to try to regress her to an earlier experience. On doing so, the girl described an incarnation in Louisiana, when as a child she saw a shadow beneath the surface just as she jumped into the water. It was an alligator, and her death was a horrible one. After returning to consciousness, she was able to understand the cause of her unreasoning fear of the shadow, which was probably cast by a low-flying bird, and went on to capture numerous diving awards. She has since gone into medicine, and is now a graduate physician who is taking her residency at a large Midwestern hospital.

One of the more remarkable aspects of prebirth regression is the ability of a subject to describe a particular life, time after time, even when put into trance by different hypnotists, and to be consistent in facts and dates. Jane Winthrop, besides describing her seeming life as a carrot-top country bumpkin, has frequently detailed a feminine incarnation as an early settler in the New World. "Never once," she says of the series of trance sessions, "have the initial scenes been duplicated. One time I was spinning yarn and gazing into an open fire of huge logs. Once I sat staring in terror at an empty water bucket, afraid to go outside to fill it. Other times I was watching my father tan cowhides, or soaking my burning feet in a cool stream, or greeting my husband who had returned from hunting, but each time I knew instantly that I was Mary Dunlap."

Jane first discovered Mary as a skinny, dark-haired girl of ten, walking down a path to church with her parents. She says that her attention was centered on her new dress made of unbleached muslin, with a high yoke and a six-inch ruffle around the bottom of the skirt. "My mother was a tall, willowy woman who held her head with dignity," Jane says. "She wore a tiny black hat perched high on a large bun of thick dark hair. My father was considerably shorter, thick-chested and somewhat stocky. Both wore somber black. A dozen or more log cabins were scattered about in no particular arrangement, and around each was a clutter of iron kettles, wooden plows, crude wheelbarrows, wagons and carts. I was somewhere near the Massachusetts coast, and it seemed that the settlement was Salem."

Moved to the age of twenty-five she said that she was now married to Allan Horton, living in a log cabin in the wilds of western Massachusetts near a small settlement called Cambria. Recalling her reaction while in trance, Jane mused: "I was consumed with terror! My eyes were riveted on a single object, an empty water bucket made of wooden staves. In the loft were our three children: Allan Jr., a slender child of six who had his father's blond hair and blue eyes; four-year-old Nancy, a beautiful youngster with curly reddish hair and dimpled cheeks; and a chunky towhead of two, whose name was Hector. All three children were fretful, and as time passed they began crying from hunger and thirst. I became aware that my own teeth were clenched to keep from screaming. The only door was barricaded, and above it hung a powder horn and musket. There was neither food nor water in the house, and I knew I had to find courage to go to the spring and the garden, even though Indians had recently burned a village and might be lurking in our woods."

Major Knight asked where her husband was, and Jane says she felt devastating loneliness as she replied that he was "away fighting Indians." He moved her ahead five years, hoping to find happier conditions, but she broke into dry, racking sobs and screamed, "He never came back! Allan never came back! The Indians!"

I have heard the tape on which this first session was recorded, and was present several years later when Jane was again regressed to Mary Dunlap, during which she repeated the same heartrending, wailing chant, "He never came back! Allan never came back!" Told to proceed to the day of her death, she said:

"I'm lying in the bed near the fireplace. It's a January night, and a blizzard's raging outside . . . an awful storm. There's a cloth over the window, and the wind billows it inward like a sail. Hector and I are alone. He's in the bed under the loft. Both of us have been too sick to take care of each other, or build a fire."

Mary (or Jane) said that she was burning with fever, and that irregular blotches of red rash dotted her thin forearms. "We had scarlet fever," she told us later, and although she has never had that disease or observed a case of it, a doctor who was present said that she had accurately described the symptoms. Told to describe her funeral, she began: "At the far end of the cabin my body lies in a rough casket that Allan Jr. made. The weather has cleared, and although Hector's still weak, he's up and dressed. Allan has come with his wife and two little boys. Nancy is here with her husband and baby. I was dead for several days before news could reach Nancy and Allan. Both of them are crying." She seemed to watch intently as three neighboring men helped Allan carry the coffin through the woods to a little church. Then, after some time had passed, she "looked down" on the churchyard, now overgrown with tall grass, and read from a rounded white headstone: "Mary Horton   Born   1723   Died 1779   May her soul rest in peace."

In various other trance sessions she identified her parents as Joel and Liza Dunlap, who had married in England and migrated to the colonies a year before her birth. Her father was a tanner, and because she objected to the foul odor which clung to his clothes, she greatly preferred her mother. She described the Anglican church made of logs, called the preacher "Parson Bartholomew," and said that "a horrible man dressed in black" would walk continuously up and down the aisle, carrying a long green sapling to which a stone was fastened by means of a leather thong. "Anyone who so much as nods during the sermons, which seem to last forever, is promptly hit on the head with this stone," she complained. She said that the benches, made of roughhewn split logs, were hard and backless.

In another scene, she saw herself and her mother making soap. "I'm cooking fat mixed with lye," she said. "Mother gets it from soaking wood ashes. It's in a big black kettle over a fire behind the cabin, and I'm stirring it with a long wooden paddle. I hate the stuff. It stinks. Everything always stinks around our place—my father, his hides, the fish, and this soap." Asked what they had to eat, she groaned, "Fish, fish, fish. Father raises corn. Mother and I pick wild berries, and we dry pumpkin. Occasionally we have venison . . . but always fish."

She told of meeting Allan Horton, who had recently come from England, at a church social, and said that they were married on June 25, 1741, when she was eighteen. "I felt tremendously thrilled to be marrying him," she later recalled. "We had a wedding feast attended by everyone in the settlement. A long table of crude boards stood in the sunshine, and on it were black iron pots of boiled venison, rabbit and wild fowl, cornbread, and pies made of dried pumpkin and molasses. The special treat was a cake mother baked of cornmeal and maple syrup. The men drank from a barrel of homemade rum and became very jolly. The women wore bright-colored dresses, and several of them sat around on stumps, nursing their babies."

Mary (or Jane) next recounted how she and her bridegroom traveled for weeks in a light wagon, pulled by a cow and an ox, to find free land. "The roads were a nightmare of stumps and rocks, and so narrow that branches kept striking our faces," she said. "We moved at a snail's pace, because the jolting was so miserable, and huge black clouds of gnats got into our nostrils and eyes. Swarms of horseflies buzzed about, and since we sometimes had nothing to shade us from the sun, the noontime heat was cruel. By late afternoon clouds of mosquitoes appeared, and when we stopped for the night Allan would hunt for a squirrel, rabbit or fowl, which we cooked over an open fire. When it rained we slept under the wagon, besieged by mosquitoes. I thought we would never reach the free land, but at last we did, and then we started building our cabin."

Under a different hypnotist, at another time, Jane dwelt upon the hardships endured by herself and the children after the Indians killed Allan. "I had to work terribly hard," she said. "We had a cow, and at first I traded butter for wool fleeces. I'd wash, card, and spin them into yarn, which I could weave at night without light. I exchanged the finished cloth for necessities and more fleeces. I had all of our clothes to make, the cow to milk and feed, the garden to tend, and the wood to chop and carry, besides cooking. I even had to do the hunting until young Allan was old enough to get deer and game. Often we had no food, when we were snowed in, and I acutely felt those hunger pangs while under hypnosis." Once, prompted by a question, she "saw" the family walking to church through the woods, young Allan leading the way with a loaded musket, sturdy Hector and pretty Nancy following, and Mary Dunlap bringing up the rear, with another loaded musket.

I asked the woman scientist to explain this strange power of the mind, which makes it possible for one to give such masses of detail about scenes and times totally unfamiliar to him, and she replied: "I have no idea. I only know that the emotions which were Mary's, and the scenes of her life seem as permanently recorded on my nervous system as anything that has happened in my present lifetime. Certainly I have never consciously known such overpowering grief as I relived each time that I spoke of Allan's death. That which comes from any of us must first be within us. When I think of that woman's hardship, her integrity and moral courage, I find myself loving and admiring her, and I am glad that the trances have mirrored for me this part of myself, which otherwise I would not have known."

Present at one of our sessions in the home of Jane Winthrop was a successful young lawyer, whose father had been a member of Franklin D. Roosevelt's presidential cabinet. He watched with amused detachment as his hostess and others submitted to hypnosis, convinced that they were faking the roles that they portrayed. His keen legal mind was far too analytical to accept a weird doctrine like reincarnation, and in order to expose the farce, he agreed to let Major Knight work on him. After exchanging some good-natured banter with friends in the room, he stretched out on the couch, and soon was recounting an episode from his childhood.

The psychologist had stressed that his mind would remain alert, so that he would afterward remember everything that had transpired while in trance. Then he instructed him to go "back back back in time" until he found himself in another physical body. At the count of twenty-five, Jim began excitedly to describe a shipwreck during a ferocious storm at sea. "It's a Norse ship. It's breaking up," he panted. "I'm clinging to a board . . . don't know whether I can hold on much longer." Moved ahead, he found that he had survived the disaster and was now living in a Norwegian village on a fjord. He continued to describe that lifetime in graphic detail, even to the loss of a hand, and upon being told that "the spirit has just left the body," he was asked to tell how he died. "A horse came galloping around a corner, pulling a cart, and ran over me," he said. "They're getting the horses out of the way now. A lady is pulling the body aside, and some men are helping her. Now it's upstairs on a bed, and my wife is crying a little. They're dressing the body in my good suit."

The hypnotist next instructed him to move along in time, until he again inhabited a different body. This time the young lawyer introduced himself as Alice Long, a fourteen-year-old girl in a small New England town called Bedford. She was dressed in a wool skirt, a blouse and shawl, and when asked to look at her house, Jim remarked in puzzled tones, "The house seems to be shut up. Oh, I see now. My parents are dead, and I've gone to live with Pastor Goodfellow at the parsonage. It's next to a white wooden church with a steeple."

At the count of five he was told that he would be fifteen years older. This time he said that he was in a two-story frame house at a seashore. Asked if he were alone, he mumbled, "People are here. There's a woman—very coarse—and several men, rough, workmen types." Asked why he (or Alice) was no longer living at the parsonage, he replied evasively, "I had to leave."

"Did you like it there?"

"Better than this."

Moved forward to the age of forty-five, the voice of Jim said, in answer to a series of questions, "I've got more money now. No, I'm not married. Yes, I'm a prostitute, if you insist." At this point, his conscious mind apparently reacted with shock to something that was transpiring, and he exclaimed, "Get me out of here! Bring me out of this damned trance. . . ."

The psychologist told him to relax, and said that at the count of twenty-five he would be fully conscious. At the end of the countdown, the attorney slowly sat up and stared at friends in the room. "Those were the most horrible men I've ever seen," he shuddered. "What a hell of a life!"

Another member of the group, who also seemingly changed gender for the present lifetime, is the wife of an executive with International Business Machines in Los Angeles. Under hypnosis she gave a wealth of detail about an incarnation as a young Boston lawyer who was gassed while fighting in France during World War I, and died from the effects of it in 1924. Marion said that she (as Thomas A. McMahon) was born in a Boston suburb, lived in a white house with a big porch, and remembered her father walking down the street each morning to work as the village postmaster.

She said that she was graduated from law school in 1903, and two years later married Marjorie Chatsworth, "a sensible girl whom I've known for a long time." She said the ceremony was performed in the Congregational church, after which the honeymooning couple went by train to the mountains in New Hampshire. Thomas (or Marion) said that his law office was in a gray stone building with a Gothic doorway, "in downtown Boston on Hill Street." Asked to mention one of his cases, Thomas said that he had successfully represented an elderly gentleman named Lucas, who was suing the city of Boston because he was injured in a fall on an icy pavement. He said that he himself was constantly ailing, after being gassed during the war, and died in 1924.

The hypnotist asked Marion only one further question: "Now that you are preparing to be reborn, why have you decided to change gender in this life?"

"Softness," she replied. Apparently she had seen so much violence in the war, as an infantryman, that she wanted to develop the softer side of her nature.

A particularly interesting hypnotic regression was that of Lance Farber, a devout Catholic, who had looked on with increasingly grave concern while his wife and others detailed strange lifetimes which they claimed to have been their own. At last he said that he would be a subject, adding, "I certainly don't believe in reincarnation, but I can't figure it out, and I'd like to see what I would say under hypnosis."

Major Knight instructed him to speak only English, as he does all of his subjects in order not to lose contact with them while they are in trance. He began the countdown, and after reaching twenty-five the room was still, except for Lance's heavy breathing. Then, in heavy guttural tones wholly unlike his own, Lance Farber slowly identified himself as Heinrich Brockton, a German dressed in brown knee breeches, white shirt, and high-topped boots laced with leather thongs. He said that the nearest town was Herchandt, on the Rhine, and that he was a self-made success who had been orphaned at the age of fourteen. He was now married and had two sets of twins, "all hollerin' at once." His wife's real name was Helma, but he called her Babe, and the crops were good.

"We own thousands of acres," he boasted, and with overbearing arrogance added, "We took 'em. Them that couldn't pay, we took." With a crafty half-smile, he explained, "Oh, it's legal. Them that borrow money gotta pay it back."

Lance's wife and sister looked at each other in bewilderment. "Why, he doesn't sound a thing like himself," Laura Farber whispered. "That grammar! Lance is a college graduate!"

Major Knight asked "Heinrich Brockton" whom he meant by "we," and the voice replied, "Me and my father-in-law. He's smart, but I can't trust him. He could hide behind a corkscrew." Art suggested that he go forward to the age of thirty, and asked if he had any more children. "Ja, eight," Brockton grunted. "Every time I go to bed I get two more." Told to repeat their names, he began, "Gertrude, Gretchen . . ." then stopped, as if too bored to continue the subject. He said that he frequently went to the bank in Herchandt to foreclose mortgages, and that he had sixty or seventy people working for him.

"Do you pay them well?" the hypnotist asked.

"Hah," he replied, with a humorless sneer. "Why pay 'em? Their job's to produce crops for me. But I feed 'em good." He identified the time as July 1763, and when asked to move ahead a few years, he said he still lived on the same land, but had built a bigger house, and that his holdings were even larger. In rough, cruel tones he told of acquiring title to all of his father-in-law's interest, following a crop failure, and said that the latter was subsequently gored to death by a bull.

"A prize bull?" the major asked.

"It surprised him all right," Heinrich chortled, with a play on words.

The arrogant German seemed shaken only once, when the hypnotist asked if all of his children had survived. Now his words came slowly, as he told of twin girls who were trampled to death by runaway horses. "A corn husker was in the field with a team," he said sadly, "and one horse stepped on a snake that bit him. He panicked. He was a good horse, but when one panics the other goes."

"What kind of snake was it?"

"We call 'em vipers. Don't let one bite ya. They're orange and black with a ferocious-lookin' face . . . get to be several feet long." He said the eleven-year-old daughters had "come lookin' for me in the fields," and that they were "as purty as speckled birds, just like their mama."

To take Heinrich's mind off the tragedy, Major Knight asked him about recreation, and he said, "I hunt wild boar and go fishin'. Catch pickerel—a black fish like gar. Mean little bastards, but awful good eatin'." The hypnotist inquired about the type of gun, and he quickly responded, "A single-shot flint. Don't get in the way of it. It'll bring a boar down in one shot." Asked how he could reload in time if he merely wounded a boar, Heinrich laughed. "Ever see a man climb a tree fast?"

Instructed to go to the last day of his life, Heinrich described having a heart attack in the field at the age of sixty-seven. He said his body was placed in a family crypt at the foot of a bluff, and that on it was carved: "Here's to the man who could raise corn and hell to match." Asked whether he liked such an epitaph, he roared, "God damn right, I do."

"What are you going to do now?"

"I'm goin' to stick around and see what my neighbor's up to. I can still bother him. He's superstitious." For a moment we thought that we had found a poltergeist, but then the voice said, "He has enough troubles. I go. A crypt's no place for a spirit."

Major Knight moved him ahead in time, to ask what he had learned from that life. In a voice heavy with regret, he said, "I stripped too many people of their land. I was always taught that if you strike a deal, do it with an iron hand. If you can't do it with one blow, bring both hands down together. Now I must prove that I can deal fairly with people."

As Lance returned to consciousness, his wife and sister were discussing the incredible contrast between Heinrich and the scrupulously honest banker they now knew him to be. Lance himself was badly shaken by the experience. At first he sat as if dazed, then started talking compulsively. "You see pictures, don't you! That corn was as high as this ceiling. The horses were bigger than those that used to pull beer wagons. Heavy Percherons, I guess; thick, long manes and tails, and thick hair over their hooves. The inside of that bank in Germany is still as clear as this room. I keep seeing a poor peasant pleading with me to give him just one more week before I foreclosed his mortgage."

He lapsed into an unhappy silence, apparently reviewing the unscrupulous Heinrich character, and finally exclaimed, "Wow! Am I glad to have another chance now!"

V

Fact or Fantasy?

FEW people seem more vibrant and thoroughly "alive" than Sam Sneed, a cocky young gambler who swaggered his way across the continent in 1872, cheating the "local yokels" and hopping trains one jump ahead of the sheriff. He was admittedly a cardshark, but a likable cuss, and as he frequently said of himself, "What talent!"

My introduction to Samuel S. Sneed occurred in California on January 22, 1968, some fifteen minutes after a cultured, well-educated young woman stretched out on a couch and dutifully followed a hypnotist's instruction to let herself drift "back back back in time." The volunteer subject was Barbara Larson, who with her scientifically trained husband lives in Palos Verdes Estates near Los Angeles. The former Barbara Frymier was graduated from Indiana University in 1949, and taught school in Fort Wayne, Indiana, until her marriage. Now the mother of three children, she is a free-lance photographer in her spare time.

I met Barbara at the home of Jane Winthrop, a scientist who is also an accomplished hypnotist. First regressed to the beginning of her present lifetime in 1927, Barbara vividly described how the attending physician handed her to her grandmother, and then to her ebullient young father, who "chuckled and hummed" as he strode back and forth across the room at the Frymiers' house in Albion, Indiana.

Then, on being told to go farther back in time until she was in a different body from the present one, she abruptly assumed the mannerisms and speaking characteristics of a young man, as she exclaimed, "Those stupid yokels . . . thinking they can play cards! Carl and I really cleaned 'em. There's a lot of gravy to be ladled from these gentlemen." In response to questions she gave her name as Sam Sneed, her age as nineteen, and the place as Wyoming. The year was 1872. Told to describe her attire, the hypnotized subject gloated, "I'm a pretty fancy dresser, y'know. I've got on a checkered suit and vest. My boots could stand a little shine, but I don't have time now. Gotta catch this train outa town."

Jane Winthrop next regressed Barbara to the age of nine, and this time she spoke like a little boy, saying that she lived in New York City, but did not know where her parents were. Told to ask her grandmother, she paused as if listening, before replying, "Granny says how many times I told you they ain't here. Now stop askin' me." Asked to write her name and her school on a piece of paper, she licked the pencil repeatedly while laboriously writing, in large childish script, "Sammy Sneed. Twented." She pronounced the school like "twentieth," but obviously could not spell it.

Moved ahead five years and told to describe her surroundings, she said, "Charlie and I are playin' cards with some men in the stable back of the hotel. They think I'm just a young punk, 'cause I play it dumb, but they're the dumb ones. Charlie and I've got signals." Asked to demonstrate some of her card signals, the refined young woman drew a finger slyly alongside her nose to indicate that she held an ace, stroked her chin to designate a queen, pulled her right ear for a king, and scratched her head for a five.

Again moved ahead in time, she boasted, "You wouldn't believe it, but I'm livin' in the hotel now. I've gone up considerably in the world. My room's not much—it's next to the kitchen—but I don't spend much time there anyhow." Queried about Charlie, she sneered, "He don't have sense enough to want to better himself. Charlie's a nice enough feller, but he's satisfied back in that stable where he's been since the year one. There's a whole big world out there, and you gotta think big." Sam claimed that he was now a big-time operator, and when Jane Winthrop asked what he was selling, the supersalesman took over in a rush. "You name it, I've got it," he bragged. "If I don't have it, I can get it for you. I got plenty of connections. Whatdaya wanna buy? How much money you got to invest?"

Trying to suppress her laughter, Jane suggested six hundred acres in Kansas. "Oh, you want wheatland," Sam said. "Better take six hundred forty acres; that'll give you a section." Jane next mentioned oil land, and Sam snapped, "Well, make up your mind. Which you want? Oil's the big thing. I got some sweet property in Pennsylvania, but you better act quick, 'cause it's goin' fast. Did you ever stop to think how much kerosene is bein' used in lamps alone, and they're findin' more uses for kerosene ever' day. Now, how much money you wanna invest? C'mon across to the saloon, and while you're gettin' a bite to eat I'll step over to City Hall and see my friend about some Pennsy oil land. I got good connections."

Apparently the only way to escape from the clutches of the high-pressure salesman was to move him forward in time; so Jane Winthrop told Sam to go to the day that he was leaving New York for Wyoming. It soon developed that he was cramming his fancy suits into "a brown paper box" and scramming over to Jersey City, to catch a train West. He seemed in such a hurry that Jane asked if the police were after him, and he huffily retorted, "Say, do you just go round askin' casual acquaintances if they're in trouble with the police? Maybe you're the one that's in trouble." After Jane managed to calm him down, he conceded that some of his deals had failed to live up to customers' expectations, and he was putting some distance between himself and the long arm of the law.

Sam's account of the trip West sounded so realistic that Jane and I both felt as if we were fellow passengers. His money was running low by the time he reached Ohio, so he left the train to hunt up a card game, but soon complained, "These stupid farmers . . . suspicious damn peasants! They don't trust Easterners." Asked to give the name of the town, Sam replied, "Don't have time to look at the signs. I'm catchin' the B & O. Those suspicious damn bastards!" Throughout the remainder of the trip, Sam continued to grouse about "these dismal little towns," and "these suspicious rubes," but on reaching San Francisco his mood turned to exhilaration. "A smart feller like me's got to operate in the big town," he gloated. "A stranger stands out too much in hick towns."

Sam Sneed seemed to be prospering in Frisco, and when Jane asked if he was working now or just playing cards, he expostulated, "You don't call that work, with those guys sittin' around the table, guns in their holsters, just waitin' to catch you up!" Sam said he was also a promoter and speculator, and when I murmured that he sounded like quite an entrepreneur, he exclaimed, "Say that again! Entrepreneur [rolling it off his tongue]. Say, that's a pretty dandy word. I gotta remember that!"

The next time that Jane moved Barbara forward in time, Sam claimed to be living in the capital at Sacramento, "where the power is." Seemingly a little surprised at himself, he confided, "You won't believe it, but I'm playin' it straight here. I'm a pretty solid citizen, by God, and folks respect me." He said he had opened up an office, Sneed's Land Properties, on N Street, and was living a couple of blocks away on L Street, at the Sacramento Hotel. "Finest red brick building in town. You can't miss it," he boasted, when we asked how to find it.

Sam said that around 1888 he had begun selling advertising for the Sacramento *Bee* because its proprietor lacked flair and was running an ad for Smith's Undertaking Establishment in a lower corner of the front page. "Now, who wants to see a mortuary ad on the front page?" he asked with some asperity. "Be different if it was Maizie's Palace of Pleasure." Asked if the *Bee* also carried ads for a girlie place like that, he chuckled, "Very discreet ones. Just 'Maizie's, Free Lunches.' " With infinite detail, Sam discussed the places and people that he knew, like Jake's Harness Shop, the Emporium, the saloon in the Sacramento Hotel, Mayor Joe Calp, and the girls at Maizie's.

Moved ahead a few years, he claimed that he was now writing editorials for the *Bee*, and when Jane expressed surprise that "an uneducated fellow like you can write," Sam exploded, "I've got two good eyes, two ears and two feet, and I bought myself a dictionary. You don't learn everything in school. I've been around, and I've learned a lot. There's a whole world out there, y'know. I began to realize that there's power in the printed word. I'll tell you, it's not something to be trifled with. We do a lot of molding with those editorials." Asked whether he signed his articles, he shrugged. "Everybody knows who I am. I tell you, I'm a power in this community."

From small-time gambler, Sam Sneed claimed to have progressed to such a "solid citizen" that he and the editor were now exposing corruption. "I'm also writin' a lot of funny stuff; got a great sense of humor," he bragged. "My God, but I've got talent! A smart young feller like me can get along without school learnin'. I always figured I can do anything the other feller can. All you need's a dictionary."

At this point, Jane Winthrop was summoned briefly from the room, and before leaving she took Barbara by the arm and told her to rest quietly until she returned. I used this opportunity to check on the tape recorder, and when I subsequently glanced at Barbara, she was lying on the sofa with her right arm held straight above her body. Realizing that Jane had inadvertently left it like that, I said, "Barbara, you can take your arm down." There was no response; so after about thirty seconds I again remarked, "Sam, lay your arm down at your side." Barbara made no move, and it was obvious that she could take instructions from no one but the person who had hypnotized her. She remained in that position, with her arm thrust skyward, until Jane returned after ten more minutes.

By this time, Barbara had been under hypnosis for nearly two hours; so, as soon as Jane returned and had her drop the arm, she took her forward to the last day of her life as Sam Sneed, asking, "What is the first thing you did today?"

"Peed," Sam responded inelegantly.

While we fought to control our laughter, Sam said that he ate breakfast in the hotel restaurant, and then walked out on the sidewalk. Breaking in on a long pause, Jane prodded, "What happened next?"

Raising up off the couch, the subject shouted, "The dirty bastard shot me!"

"Why?" Jane asked, in a shocked tone.

"Something I'd written about him."

"Corruption? Was it true?"

"So help me God, it was true," Sam said convincingly.

Encouraged to tell about his funeral, Sam declared, "Everybody in town came, and all the girls from Maizie's, in all their finery. What a way to go! What a funeral!" Asked to recall what the pastor said at the services, Sam mimicked, "Sam Sneed was a g-r-e-a-t citizen . . . a great Christian."

Breaking into raucous laughter, he bellowed, "My God, can you imagine me—a great Christian? The dirty pious parson. That lousy Methodist parson. Why, he's just as crooked as I am, and he knows it. He'll get his come-uppance. Sam Sneed, a great Christian! I coulda died laughing."

Queried as to where he was during the funeral, Sam chortled. "For awhile I was sittin' right up on that ol' pine box. I laughed so hard I coulda died. They all pulled long faces over 'poor old Christian Sam.' I must say I looked pretty good in that box. Fortunately, the guy didn't spoil my face when he shot me. Shot a nice hole in my chest, but the undertaker did a good job of fixin' me up, and it didn't show. I had on a checkered vest, but I'd become more discreet, and thank God I'd gotten a black suit. I did look substantial!"

Asked if he recommended funerals, he chortled, "You don't wanna miss it. Best party I ever went to. All of 'em talkin' about good old Sam, and you know those lousy bastards cheated me at cards every time, and then pulled those long faces." Sam said he was buried "just across the river" in the Sacramento cemetery, and that his tombstone read, "In reverent memory of Samuel S. Sneed, by his friends. 1896."

Jane Winthrop asked if he left a will, and Sam replied, "Well, I should say a good, well-educated man like me did have a will. I left everything to Maizie's Palace of Pleasure, 'for the edification of their spirits.' By Jesus, they laughed at that!"

"Did you leave very much?" Jane prodded.

"Well, I left everything I had to Maizie. I didn't have much cash, but there's a fair amount of land, and when they get that real estate office settled up, Maizie oughta come out real well. The way land values are goin' up, I'd say it was a good-sized fortune, if Maizie holds onto the land; say fifteen or twenty thousand dollars."

Sam said that after the funeral he went "with the boys" back to the saloon at the hotel, where the bartender set up a round of drinks, and they toasted, "To Sam, rest in peace." Conceding that he was "rather moved" by the tributes, he said, "I was a real honest person in that town, by God. The only honest thing I ever did, so by Jesus don't make fun of it." Asked why he never married, he said, "Well, if Maizie'd been the marryin' kind, and I'd been the marryin' kind, we'd probably have got married, but we were just friends. Besides [with a chuckle] I couldn't see givin' it all to one."

Jane asked Sam why he had reformed in later years, and he replied, "It was just too damn easy . . . no challenge anymore. It was so easy to take advantage of those poor, deluded, uneducated dopes that after a time it was no fun anymore. It was more of a challenge to be honest."

Barbara was then instructed to go forward in time, in order to appraise that lifetime as Sam Sneed and tell its purpose. "It wasn't wasted," she began slowly. "But do you realize that I spent nearly my entire life preying on the stupidity of other people for my own advantage! Only toward the end did I realize that it was more fun to be honest than crooked. Then I really got smart, but I only had a few years to try to rectify all those misdeeds. It took me almost forty years to realize that it's not so smart to gyp people; that it's better to bring out their goodness than to harp on their stupidity."

Jane asked what souls do between lives, and the voice of Barbara continued, "You have to evaluate, to weigh the past life and formulate what it is that you'll need, and what you'll seek in the next one." Asked what she was coming back to learn, she replied, "Now I must learn to love."

"Why did you choose to be born a woman this time?" Jane continued.

"Because I hadn't used women very well in that life," she replied.

"What other lesson did you learn as Sam, that you can profit by in your life as Barbara?"

"It's got to be hard. If it's too easy, you don't grow. If your whole life is easy, you never learn. You just don't get involved in the nitty-gritty." And with that, Jane slowly brought Barbara out of trance.

To watch the transformation of swaggering, boastful Sam Sneed into a charming, attractive California matron was an astonishing experience. For two hours I had been so caught up in the life of this Personality Kid that I felt I knew him better than most of my friends, because this seemed to be the inner man speaking. Those who have since heard the tape recording capture this same intensity of feeling, and roar with laughter at his brash sallies.

It was therefore with an uncomfortable sense of spying on an old friend that I wrote to Eugene Hill, managing editor of the Sacramento *Bee*, to ask if he would check out some of the assertions. I did not tell him why I wanted to know, but he was admirably cooperative, and his subsequent letter sounded like a second funeral for Samuel S. Sneed. He said that there was no record of a Sacramento Hotel on L Street, where Sam had placed it, or on any other street. The City Directory of that era listed no Sam Sneed, which could have been understandable if he lived in a hotel, but it also failed to show a Joe Calp. The city library's records make no mention of Jake's Harness Shop, or of Smith's Undertaking Establishment; the city cemetery has no listing of a Sam Sneed burial, and the *Bee* has no knowledge of his having worked there seventy years ago.

What, then, is the explanation? Certainly Barbara did not deliberately manufacture for herself a previous lifetime as a cardshark and uneducated braggadocio. Sam Sneed's pursuits were totally alien to Barbara's refined upbringing in the conservative atmosphere of a small Midwestern town and college campus, and so far as she is aware she had neither read nor seen movies of a character who approximates Sam's life story. She may possibly have learned in grammar school that a section of land comprises six hundred and forty acres, but she is confident that if someone had asked her for that information before she was hypnotized, she could not have supplied it. The total personality change which she underwent while "reliving" Sam Sneed was as dramatically different from her own as were the tone of voice, the vernacular and profanity. There is no question but that she was hypnotized, since a conscious person would find it remarkably uncomfortable to hold his arm above his head for nearly fifteen minutes—although it did not bother her in the least—and her explosive indignation at being shot by a swindler was worthy of a Sarah Bernhardt performance, if it was feigned.

A number of years ago, Barbara lived for a few months in an outlying suburb of Sacramento, but was so busily occupied with two small children that she went downtown only twice; and if she had been drawing on her conscious memory, she would not have made so many errors about streets and places. A more likely explanation is that having once lived in Sacramento as Barbara, she subconsciously placed the locale for Sam Sneed's life there also, whereas the events described may have actually transpired in some other city.

Baffled by our inability to solve the riddle, I questioned several eminent psychiatrists who have worked with hypnotic regression. They ascribed such errors to three possible conditions:

1. A subject, anxious to respond to the questioning of a hypnotist, may subconsciously identify with someone he has read or heard about, and fabricate details much as we make up stories to tell the children.

2. While in hypnotic trance, the subject may be temporarily taken over by an earthbound entity, and used as a medium to tell a boastful story.

3. The subject may actually be reliving one of his own previous incarnations, but the entity may try to make himself sound more glamorous or successful than the facts warrant. Many investigators of the Bridey Murphy case believe that this is the explanation for some of her patently false assertions, and that she was wistfully trying to make an exceedingly drab life sound more important.

The psychiatrists suggested rehypnotizing Barbara, without telling her of the errors, so that Sam Sneed could be confronted with the inconsistencies in his story. This was done, and on being regressed to a previous lifetime, Barbara surprised us by first describing an incarnation as Richard Stephenson, a farm boy in New York State, who died in 1811 at the age of twelve, when a team of horses bolted and crushed him against a tree.

The hypnotist then instructed Barbara to move forward in time until she found herself in another body, and at the count of twenty-five she cockily identified herself as Sam Sneed, gave her age as thirty-seven, and said that she was wearing black shoes, a black coat and "fine-striped gray-blue trousers." When asked the color of the hair, Sam laughed uproariously and replied, "Brownish."

"What's so funny?" Jane Winthrop prompted.

"Wellllll," Sam chuckled, "there's not a whole lot of it up there anymore. But I'm pretty good-looking." He said that he was presently in a small upstate California town to negotiate for some land. "I deal in property," he explained grandly. "Up here I've been buying farmland. There's a lot of other land that's mighty rocky and has pine trees on it, but I can't get anyone interested in developing it for lumber." Sam said that he worked out of Sacramento, and when there lived at the Grand Hotel. He admitted that he sometimes used a marked deck when playing cards with "a regular bunch of gentlemen," but when asked how he marked the cards, he snapped, "I really don't think that's any of your business."

(Editor Eugene Hill later confirmed that in the 1890's there was a Grand Hotel on K Street.)

Sam became rather incensed when challenged about some of his earlier claims. He insisted that they were true and stuck closely to the original story, but supplied a few additional details. He gave the "local madam's" name as Maizie Moller (a phonetic spelling, since he merely pronounced it), and said that he was fatally shot on May 11, 1896, by Frank Jordan, a rancher. "I fingered him out in a dirty deal," he averred, when asked why Jordan killed him. "He was pulling a dirty deal, buying up land under another name and taking advantage of the government, and I exposed him." He indicated that he was not on the payroll of the Sacramento *Bee,* but occasionally contributed articles under various pseudonyms, "and people knew I wrote 'em."

Informed that the city cemetery had no record of his burial, he uttered a surprised "hmmmmm," and insisted that he could see his gravestone. "It's kinda toppled over on one side, and the cemetery looks abandoned," he mused. "The marker is nearly overgrown with vines, but you can still read 'In reverent memory' on it." With that, he again broke into loud laughter, as if remembering all of those funeral tributes to him as "a good Christian."

Sam Sneed seems entirely too real to be shrugged off as a flight of fancy. He may have boasted too much about his reformation and status as a solid citizen, but those who have seen Barbara under hypnosis, or heard the tape recordings, are convinced that a witty cardshark named Sam Sneed once lived, breathed, and had his being. Sacramento may not have been the place where he cavorted, but perhaps a reader of this book may be able to supply the missing clue.

VI

Between Lives

A PROMINENT psychiatrist who has regressed more than a hundred patients through hypnosis, during the past ten years, reports that most "good subjects" can talk as easily about the period "between lives" as about former earthly incarnations; and that despite widely disparaging religious and cultural backgrounds, all give approximately the same description of the "spirit world."

"In many cases they express great joy at being dead," he said, "stressing the marvelous feeling of being so much more free and 'alive' than when in the physical body. On one occasion I remarked to a hypnotized subject, 'Now that you're dead, how do you feel?' and she heatedly protested, 'You're the dead one, not me.'"

The psychiatrist said that as soon as he utters some such phrase as "Now that the soul has left the body," the subject will usually tell the reason for the life just lived, saying, "I had to learn to be less selfish," or "I had to experience unkindness so that I could know how important kindness is." When asked the overall purpose of earthly life, the answer often is, "To learn to love," or "To become more Christ-like and thoughtful of others."

"Perhaps the subject has described a life in which he was an atheist, or a nonchurchgoer," the hypnotist continued, "but immediately upon being told that 'the soul has now left the body,' that same person will answer my questions by saying, 'Of course I believe in God. Everyone believes in God. God is!" When asked about the meaning of the term Old Souls, their answer invariably is that such an entity has incarnated many, many times, thus acquiring considerable wisdom; whereas a Young Soul, having had fewer earthly lives, still has many lessons to learn. The subjects usually stress that agewise, however, everyone is the same, having existed since the beginning. I have questioned some of them about so-called guardian angels, and they reply that we all have many of them, and that they may vary depending upon the particular problem at hand. For instance, a woman who is fearful of childbirth will be surrounded by guardian angels who, during their own earthly lifetimes, also feared childbirth but had normal deliveries. A person who wants to kick the alcohol habit, and prays for help, will be surrounded by souls who successfully overcame the problem. The value of prayer is repeatedly stressed, the idea being that the more prayers that are devoutly offered, the more guardian angels will come to help; and that they are nothing more than souls like ourselves, but between lives.

"I have often asked hypnotized subjects about ghosts, and have received similar answers. Ghosts, they indicate, are of two varieties: a close relative or friend who comes to warn of an impending danger, or someone who has died violently, and not realizing that he has passed over, will remain to 'haunt' the premises that he knew.

"My regressed patients say that the same souls return together time and again, as friends, relatives and enemies; and that we can earn the right to choose our own parents. One young woman kept telling me 'between lives' that she wanted to be born again, and when I asked what was preventing it, she said her mother wasn't yet born. She had placed the time as approximately 1880, and a subsequent check showed that her mother was not born until after that date. I am convinced that everyone who can be regressed through hypnosis will describe as many lives as one wishes to delve into, but the surprising aspect is that the subjects seldom contradict themselves. One of my subjects has described more than twenty past lives, and never once has there been a discrepancy in dates, so that one life overlapped another."

I asked the psychiatrist whether he agrees with some critics who claim that regressed persons fabricate stories in order to please the hypnotist or build up their own egos, and he replied: "Not in my experience. Many of the subjects suffer excruciatingly, and describe dreary lives which could only deflate their egos." This would certainly seem to be true in the case of the well-known attorney, a non-believer in reincarnation, who nevertheless described a life as a prostitute under hypnosis, and was so shocked by the experience that he afterward had nightmares about it. It would also be true of the woman who shriekingly told of having been hung for stealing, and of the French one who said she was beheaded because she was found in a hotel bedroom with her British lover.

The psychiatrist added that some subjects speak in foreign tongues of which they have no conscious knowledge, and many describe settings and situations which are simply beyond their normal ken. He cited as an example the case of Jane Winthrop, who when describing the life of Mary Dunlap, said that at her wedding feast a number of women were sitting around on stumps, nursing their babies. "It stretches our imagination to believe," he said, "that a woman of the caliber of Jane Winthrop would have deliberately 'created' such a strange scene as a part of a wedding celebration."

Among the more intriguing aspects of hypnotic regression is the spiritual philosophy which pours from the lips of an entranced subject when instructed to discuss the state "between lives," or to appraise the incarnation that he has seemingly relived. In his normal state he may be rather inarticulate, but under hypnosis he speaks with calm assurance in this phase of the regression. And whether or not the subjects believe in reincarnation and God, the philosophy neatly dovetails. To cite two typical examples:

While visiting Jane Winthrop in California early in 1968, I met two young women with highly dissimilar backgrounds. Beautiful, vivacious Vickey Hinchman is happily married to the president of Research Development Manufacturing Company of Culver City, California, and is an extremely well-adjusted person. Helen Macon, on the other hand, had a decidedly unhappy childhood, is in the process of obtaining a divorce, and is a schoolteacher.

Helen Macon forthrightly declared that the doctrine of reincarnation is for the birds. She was emphatic in arguing that neither she nor anyone else had ever occupied more than one physical body, and perhaps to prove her point she agreed to let Jane Winthrop try to hypnotize her. Stretching out on the sofa in the study, Helen closed her eyes and concentrated on the instructions as Jane soothingly told her, "You will go back back in time, until at the count of twenty-five you can tell us about the body in which you find yourself. Your mind will remain sharp and clear, and afterward you will remember everything that happens. Now relax. One, two, three. . . ."

At the count of twenty-five, Jane briskly suggested that she describe herself, and Helen, with a childish lisp totally unlike her own assertive voice, whimpered, "My feet hurt."

"Why do your feet hurt?" Jane asked.

"They've bound them, so they won't grow big and ugly like my amah's," she explained. Then, in answer to questions, she said that she was three years old, and she gave her Chinese name and the city where she lived. Moved fifteen years ahead in time, she said that she was now married to a man whom her father had chosen "because he's very rich." Asked if they had children, she replied, "No, I am barren. But I don't care. I hate my husband. He's horrible to me."

A little later, her bitterness turned to elation as she told of being carried by coolies to a teahouse, where she was to have a rendezvous with her lover. "I'm not supposed to go there," she whispered in conspiratorial tones, "but he sent a message for me to come. He has paid off the coolies, and the woman who owns the teahouse will give us privacy." Advanced to the closing hours of that life, Helen broke into racking sobs, saying, "I'm frightened. I'm so frightened! He has put a cup of tea in front of me, and I have to drink it. Ohhhh, I'll never see my beautiful little son again."

"Why are you afraid?" Jane prodded. "I thought you couldn't have children, by the way."

Trying to suppress the sobs which by now were nearly choking her, Helen replied, "I wasn't barren at all. I had a baby, but it wasn't my husband's." Under continued questioning, the story gradually took form. After she discovered her pregnancy, loyal servants told her husband that she was too ill for him to see, and when her condition could no longer be concealed, they helped her to escape to a house in the mountains. Then they informed her husband that she had contracted leprosy, and had gone to a leper colony to avoid infecting him. For the past nine years, she had been happily living in the mountain abode with a servant and her little boy, whose natural father came frequently to visit.

Asked what had now gone awry, she wailed, "I was a fool. I trusted my sister. I wanted something from my former home—a little ivory carving that my lover once gave me. I had buried it in the garden, and when a servant came with provisions, I asked him to go there and dig it up for me. I had told him to tell my sister, but you can't trust her. She's cruel! She doesn't have a lover."

The sister, she said, had told her father and husband, who came to the mountains and surprised her and her lover. The latter was permitted to leave with their nine-year-old son. Then her father told a servant to bring a cup of tea, "and I'm so frightened," she gasped. "My father is putting a white powder in it. Now it's in front of me. I have to drink it. I'll never see my beautiful little son again." A moment later, having apparently drunk the deadly potion, she began moaning, "My bowels are burning." Her physical torment was so apparent that Jane quickly came to the rescue, saying, "Now the spirit has left the body. You will feel no more pain. Tell us what happened. Do you hate your father for making you drink poison?"

"Oh, no," she replied, in a sweetly submissive voice. "They felt that they were doing the right thing. I can see into my father now, and he loves me, but he had to do it because I had disgraced them." Jane asked if the family had made no attempt to visit her at the leper colony all those nine years that they thought she was there, and she replied, "Of course not. You don't go there. I never went there. You'd get leprosy!" She identified the year of her death as 1757.

Jane Winthrop next told Helen that she would come forward in time until she found herself "in another body." Helen seemed to doze during the count to twenty-five, but when Jane completed it and asked if her feet hurt, she replied gaily, "Of course not. They're bare." She said that she was a little girl of nine, in a red and white dress, "running running running in the woods," and that her name was Nancy Woods.

"What country are you in?" Jane asked.

"Missouri," she replied.

"What year is it?"

"Eighteen nineteen."

Taken forward to the age of twenty-five, Nancy Woods said that her last name was now Johnson. She had been married since she was sixteen, and had four children. Asked what her husband did for a living, she responded, "Works on the plantation, of course." Jane said she had never heard of a plantation in Missouri, and Nancy retorted positively, "Well, we're on a plantation." She paused and then added, "It isn't ours, you know."

"Oh? Do you have Negroes to help with the crops?" Jane asked.

"Why, we're Negroes," she said matter-of-factly.

"Oh! Is your hair kinky?"

"Of course!"

Nancy (or Helen) identified the plantation owner as "Mr. Langley," and insisted that this was his full name, until she finally recalled having heard "white folks" call him Thomas. She said he called his wife Caroline, and that they had children named Caroline, Thomas, Dorothy and Mark. Asked the name of the nearest town, she replied indifferently, "I don't know. I've never been there."

Nancy was supposedly twenty-five years old at this time, but she had no recollection of having heard the name of the place where the Langleys bought provisions that they did not produce on the property. Jane therefore instructed her to ask eleven-year-old Caroline Langley; and after a pause, during which she seemed to be carrying on a private conversation, Nancy said, "She says it's Jackson." Jane told her to find out what county Jackson was in, and this time Nancy replied with some anxiety, "She asks me, 'What's the matter with you? You crazy or something? Why do you need to know?' " Instructed to go into the big house and ask some of the grown-ups, Nancy was quiet for a time, and then burst forth, "They all look at me like I'm crazy for asking. They won't answer me."

While regressed to her childhood, Nancy had said that she envied the white children in some ways, but not in others. "They have such beautiful clothes, and ride in carriages, and have such beautiful food," she sighed. Prodded to tell in what way she did not envy the Langley children, she exclaimed, "The little girls can't go without shoes. They have to have their hair brushed and curled, and ribbons put in it. They have to take care of their dresses to keep clean. They can't wade barefoot in the creek and run in the woods like I do. I love to run in the woods."

At the age of twenty-five, her conversation with the hypnotist went like this:

"Are you a slave?"

"Yes, of course."

"Does the master sell slaves, and could he sell you or your family?"

"He could, but he wouldn't. This is where we belong. We've always been here."

"Are your parents living there?"

"My mother is dead, and my father is very, very, very old. He doesn't have to work anymore. Mr. Langley is very kind to us."

"Do the white men ever make passes at you, Nancy?"

"Of course not. Mr. Langley is a gentleman."

Jane took Nancy to the last day of her life, and when she spoke again her voice sounded quavery with age as she said, "I'm very, very old. [*Long sigh*] Must be about ninety. I've got great-grandchildren now." She said that only three of her six children were living. Tommy and Alice had died of scarlet fever, and a baby was born dead. "But that was a long, long time ago. My husband also died. Diphtheria. But that was so long ago. So long. . . ."

She recalled that during the War Between the States, soldiers with long muskets had once come into the "kitchen and dining room, and we had to cook for them." Asked if they were enemy soldiers, she responded, "Not the enemy, but not friendly to us. They demanded anything they wanted, and put a lot of squawking chickens in gunnysacks and took them away."

After being told that her spirit had left the body, she was asked to describe her funeral, and she became unusually animated, saying, "It's a nice one. My grandchildren are standing around. Some are crying; not all of them. The little children are just interested and kind of excited about what's going on. It's not in a church, you know. It's at the edge of the woods, and they've dug a hole there to put the box in. I can see the preacher. He's colored. He has on a shirt with dark blue stripes special for the occasion, and a tie. He's holding a Bible against his chest and rocking back on his heels. He's funny to watch! He's rolling his eyes now, and saying, 'Dearly beloved, we are gathered here together.' [*Giggling*] He sounds so pompous, rolling his eyes heavenward. 'She lived a long and Christian life. She raised her children to be good Christians in the eyes of the Lord. Amen.' All the people are putting their hands on their hearts and saying, 'Amen.' Look at my little great-granddaughter—she's Nancy, too—putting her little hand on her heart after all the others did, and saying, 'Amen.' Don't you think she's pretty!"

After she had taken a last, lingering look at the funeral, Jane asked her to assess that life as Nancy, and the hypnotized subject replied, "There were lots of things about that life that were very important. I didn't really see it happen because we were happy, but there was a great deal of antagonism between the colored and white races. The Langleys treated us like people. They were kind, but I had to learn patience, of course. It was a happy kind of life, even though I worked very hard, and was in an inferior position."

Jane Winthrop then asked her to discuss the period between lives, and answer some of our questions about the cycle of rebirth. The entranced schoolteacher said that we do not necessarily have the same family each time, as our relationships with other entities are frequently reshuffled, but that we ordinarily select our parents. "I have certain obstacles that I have to overcome in order to learn," she explained, "and the parents I choose also have something to learn by having me, so it's a double attraction. Sometimes you make a mistake in your selection, but you don't need to waste that particular lifetime as a consequence. Even though you may not be able to work on the particular lessons that you intended to return for, you can be learning other things, although they're sometimes out of the expected order."

Helen said that the purpose of continued rebirth is to search for "wisdom—the complete knowing," and that meditation is extremely important to every person in order to "develop further self-knowing, and through that knowing, to find God." Asked to define God, she said, "God is the name for What Is." Told to explain the difference between prayer and meditation, she said, "The Lord's Prayer is the same as meditation. Meditation means giving our total attention to something on which our attention is focused. Prayer is different. It is not good to recite prayers that someone else has made up. The prayer that we pray today will not necessarily fit for tomorrow. We should make a fresh contact with God each time."

She told us that when we pray for help in time of danger or crisis, we "attract a tremendous force, a drawing of energies from entities who can protect us from harm, if the prayer is sincere." Answering specific questions, she said, "I'm conscious of light everywhere. I seem to be wherever I think about. Souls are all around, and of course we can communicate. How? We just know! Our greater period of development is on earth, rather than here, because there we pit ourselves against obstacles, and as we surmount them we grow in understanding. Between earthly lives we have an expanding knowingness, and after assessing the errors of our past life, we decide the kind of obstacles which will best help us to advance in the next incarnation."

She defined an Old Soul as one who "has developed further through frequent rebirths," and said, "all souls have always been, but not all of them have lived on earth, or chosen to return there very often. There are more people on earth now than ever before, because of the greater opportunity to be born. It's a purely physical thing. There are more vehicles available—more bodies; a stepping-up of tempo for development." She said that water, fire and color are essential to soul development, as well as to the physical being, but that "love is the most important thing; a selfless caring for what happens to other people as well as ourselves.

"Man began in water," she continued, "not only as amoeba in the sea but also as an embryo in water, and the cells remember. For that reason swimming is very important, and the feel of the sun on the body. These are basic elements. People need color, beauty, nature. Everything is made up of color, but with machinery, dust, ugly buildings, junk and pollution, all is turning dingy gray. People need color and solitude in order to communicate with their souls. This is tremendously important to their development. Take time to commune, time to care, and time to love."

Helen was gradually brought out of her hypnotic state, after which she lay quietly on the couch for a few minutes before observing in a tone of complete bafflement, "If there's nothing to reincarnation, where in the world did all of that come from? I simply can't understand it!"

Is it any wonder that she was puzzled? In the space of two hours, she had seemingly been a member of three races of man: yellow, black, and white.

The next day our subject was Vickey Hinchman, and after Jane Winthrop had hypnotically regressed her to "another lifetime," she said that she was living in a cave, in an area that we now call the Arctic Circle. She had apparently tuned in on a period when the earth was young, millions of years ago, because she described a tropical, marshy land that was overrun with huge beasts which "make frightful noises." Asked if she was speaking of dinosaurs, she replied, "before dinosaurs," and said that they were "enormous green monsters" whose forelegs were webbed to their bodies.

She was able to tell us of the beasts' appearance only after that life had ended, and she could look "down" at them; for she said that throughout her lifetime she never left the vast cave in which she had been born. She explained that the men had to venture outside to bring back food, including a plant that somewhat resembled today's eggplant, but that no woman was brave enough to go because of the animals, which often killed the men. Despite the limitations of cave-dwelling, Vickey described a happy life filled with love for her husband, children, parents and friends. Apparently man's only enemy then was beast, not fellowman.

Jane suggested that Vickey come considerably farther ahead in time, and at the count of twenty-five she identified herself as Japeth, a young Egyptian woman whose father, in approximately A.D. 1500, had sold her to Lander, a wealthy Arab. With an eye for vivid detail, she described a tent hung with blue and gold curtains, pitched beside an oasis, which she shared with nine other women who had similarly been purchased as wives for Lander. Asked to locate the tent more specifically, she said, "It is four days' travel from the Nile. We were carried here in silk boxes, on camels' backs."

In answer to questioning, she said, "Yes, I was glad to be sold. It will be a good life. All the women are excited. We will play together and raise our children together. The air is so clean and warm here. I like it. Father got camels and silks in exchange for me."

Moved forward in time, she told us that her husband had been killed "in a skirmish" before she ever saw him. Asked if she married again, she replied in shocked tones, "Oh no. That would have defiled us, to be sold to someone else. Our husband was wealthy. We were kept together after his death. We painted flowers. We used fruit juices for coloring."

After Jane told her that her spirit had left that body, and asked her to describe the end of the life, she said, "I died with arthritis. I couldn't paint because of the pain. I couldn't breathe. I died a quiet death. That life was a pleasant waste

. . . but a waste. It's more pleasurable if you accomplish something, and that was a barren life." Jane wanted to know what became of the body, and Vickey continued, "They have temporarily wrapped it in soft, fine gauze and are taking it in a cart. It will be wrapped again in a thick, stiff material almost like paper. The body has been emptied, emptied of everything. Why would they want to do that? What do they want with the body? They're being very gentle with it. Now it is stored in the busy pathway of an underground tunnel where there are shops, so it won't feel lonely. Other bodies are stored close by, so that none will feel lonely."

The tranquility of that life was in marked contrast to the stark horror of a much later one which Vickey next described. As the count ended, she said that she was lying in a sodden alley on the outskirts of Boston, and that cats were clawing at a garbage can into which something (the placenta?) had just been deposited. "I've just been born," she murmured. "I'm cold, cold, cold. Oh, I'm so cold!" Asked about her mother, she said, "She's going away. I see her back. She's leaving me here in the rain. I'm so cold!"

Moved forward to her death, Vickey said that she had lain in the mud and rain for nearly three days, before her spirit left the body, and that the oozing mud had felt much warmer than the air. Asked if she resented being abandoned by her mother, she replied softly, "No, she loved me, but she couldn't help what she did. Her lover had abandoned her. I've had the same mother in several lives."

Jane Winthrop asked Vickey, while between lives, to define Heaven, and she replied, "Heaven is a somethingness. A lack of a void. Our accomplishments determine whether we go there. I started out there. We all did, but I've not been there since. I haven't earned it yet."

Jane wanted to know whether souls must keep reincarnating, and the entranced young woman said, "You can quit if you want, or you can skip it entirely. You need drive and eagerness, to try for the beyondness. You can end reincarnation and stay in darkness, if you choose. It's up to each soul. Each time that we occupy a body, it's only a second in the expanse of time. We come back each time to accomplish something, to compensate for any harm that we have done to others, and to keep them from being hurt. Maybe that's the only 'natural' death; when we don't need to come back anymore."

VII

An Open Mind

REINCARNATION offers so many advantages that if more of us were to adopt the philosophy, life could take on more pleasant dimensions. Westerners who believe that we live but once seem always in a hurry, crowding each day too full of activities to have time for contemplation; whereas Orientals, confident that each lifetime is but a brief interval in the immutable cycle of return, find the leisure for such charming formalities as tea sipping and philosophical conversation.

Man's frenetic drive for power and wealth loses its attraction when he accepts the premise that the worldly emoluments acquired in one lifetime will have no value in his next one; that the only carry-overs will be the good that he has accomplished, and the evil wrought. Belief in reincarnation dispels fear of death and eases the grief of bereavement, since those loved ones who precede us in death will be encountered many times again. Strains in family relationships can be released, in understanding that the ties were forged through previous affinity or karmic relationships. Hatreds can turn into friendships, if the antagonists accept that unless they resolve their differences now, they must meet each other again under still more trying circumstances.

The philosophy of reincarnation, when properly applied to one's daily life, promotes compassion for others less fortunate; but in some Eastern cultures it is misapplied. The untouchables are a case in point. Those highborn Hindus who treat another caste as beneath contempt, arguing that they earned their lowly state through previous misdeeds, overlook the possibility that by their own callous disregard for human suffering they may be earning a similar fate in their next incarnation. Just as our deeds of yesterday can forge today's destiny, so our present conduct will determine our future fate.

Dr. Rudolf Steiner, the German anthroposophist, compared karma to sleep, remarking that just as we arise each morning to resume activities which have been conditioned by yesterday's actions, so the deeds of yesterday determine our present lot. "If I made a mistake yesterday, even though sleep intervened, I must try to rectify it today or bear the consequences," he wrote in *Reincarnation and Karma*. "Otherwise we would be created anew each day. While we sleep we are withdrawn from the field of action, but destiny or karma awaits when we waken. It is the same with karma from former incarnations. It belongs to us. The soul preserves the effects of my deeds from former lives and brings it about that the spirit, in a new incarnation, appears in the form which previous lives have given it. The spirit is eternal."

This is not to imply that all misfortunes, or physical and mental defects, relate to past misdeeds. Within the framework of universal law we have free will, and some souls may have deliberately chosen to return with afflictions in order to learn some needed lesson of humility, tolerance, or compassion. Not all babies who die from unexplained causes were denied life because they had previously taken another's. Some may so love their chosen parents that they voluntarily returned, and shortly withdrew, in order to help the parents develop understanding through such loss. Thus, if a mother proves inconsolable in her grief, failing to comfort others through the insight gained by her own heartache, she will have wasted that opportunity for soul growth.

Is the cycle of rebirth really hard to believe? Francesco Redi, a seventeenth-century Italian scientist, was considered a heretic by contemporaries because he maintained that even the lowest forms of life originate through reproduction; for the orthodox scientists of that day believed that worms, insects and even fish could originate out of lifeless mud. Redi insisted that all living creatures descended from living creatures, and two centuries later Louis Pasteur found irrefutable proof that living springs only from the life germ. Today, the spiritual scientist maintains that the soul nature can spring only from the soul, and just as everything living originates out of the living, so every soul has previously existed. The present lack of proof for this contention is not so earthshaking when we recall that man was unaware even of the existence of germs until recent times. Most of us have so little knowledge of science and mathematics that we must simply accept the thesis that the earth revolves around the sun, or that Einstein knew what he was talking about with his law of relativity, because we cannot personally document it.

Belief in reincarnation antedates scientific proof of the laws of the universe, including our revolving planetary system, by many thousands of years. It was a major tenet of Brahmanism centuries before the birth of Buddha, and the Vedantic school taught that neither the will of God nor the fault of parents formed children's characters. Rather, each child is responsible for his own capabilities, powers and character through conduct in previous lives. In the sixth century B.C., Gautama Siddhartha, a prince who was surrounded with love and wealth, renounced the world in order to understand the meaning of life. After years of privations he received illumination, and devoted the remainder of his time to teaching reincarnation and karma. This was Buddha, and one of his contemporaries was Pythagoras, the Hellenic philosopher who went to India and was initiated into the esoteric Brahman rites. The teachings of Pythagoras, who said that he remembered many of his previous lives, influenced the thinking of Plato, who taught that periodic reincarnation is necessary for the perfection of man's divine nature, and that each soul chooses his own personality and fate before rebirth.

Roman Emperor Julian believed that he had been Alexander the Great in a previous lifetime, and the Talmud states that the soul of Abel passed into the body of Seth and later into that of Moses. The Essenes of Palestine believed in reincarnation, and it was taught in the Platonic Academy of Greece for nine centuries, until Emperor Justinian closed the Academy in 529.

In more modern times the Scottish philosopher, David Hume, wrote: "The soul, if immortal, existed before our birth." Benjamin Franklin observed, "Thus, finding myself to exist in the world, I believe I shall, in some shape or other, always exist; and with all the inconveniences human life is liable to, I shall not object to a new edition of mine, hoping, however that the errata of the last may be corrected." Ralph Waldo Emerson, America's greatest philosopher, declared, "We are driven by instinct but have innumerable experiences which are of no visible value, and we may resolve through many lives before we shall assimilate or exhaust them."

Mohandas K. Gandhi wrote to Madeleine Slade, daughter of a distinguished British admiral, who became one of Gandhi's disciples: "What you say about rebirth is sound. It is nature's kindness that we do not remember past births. What is the good either of knowing in detail the numberless births we have gone through? Life would be a burden if we carried such a tremendous load of memories. A wise man deliberately forgets many things, even as a lawyer forgets the cases and their details as soon as they are disposed of. Yes, 'death is but a sleep and a forgetting.' If death is not a prelude to another life, the intermediate period is a cruel mockery."

Jesus, like Buddha, is thought to have taught an inner, higher doctrine to His immediate disciples, and this explains why they "understood that He spake unto them of John the Baptist" when He said that Elias had returned unrecognized. Tibetan Buddhists believe that their Dalai Lama is the reincarnation of Chenrezi, one of the emancipated souls who has discharged all personal karmic debts but voluntarily returns to help mankind.

Many prominent Americans have not only professed their belief in reincarnation, but have seemed to recapture memories of their past lives. Henry David Thoreau wrote in *Letters and Journals*: "I have lived in Judea eighteen hundred years ago, but I never knew that there was such a one as Christ among my contemporaries. And Hawthorne, too, I remember as one with whom I sauntered in old heroic times along the banks of the Scamander amid the ruins of chariots and heroes. As the stars looked to me when I was a shepherd in Assyria, they look to me now a New Englander. As far back as I can remember I have unconsciously referred to the experiences of a previous state of existence."

Louisa May Alcott wrote in a letter: "I think immortality is the passing of a soul through many lives or experiences; and such as are truly lived, used, and learned help on to the next, each growing richer, happier and higher, carrying with it only the real memories of what has gone before. . . . I seem to remember former states and feel that in them I have learned some of the lessons that have ever since been mine here, and in my next step I hope to leave behind many of the trials I have struggled to bear here and begin to find lightened as I go on. This accounts for the genius and great virtue some show here. They have done well in many phases of this great school and bring into our class the virtue or the gifts that make them great or good."

In *Song of Myself,* Walt Whitman wrote that he tramped a perpetual journey, and "no doubt I have died myself ten thousand times before." Mark Twain wrote of a recurring dream in which, over a period of forty years, he "knew" the same girl in various eras, localities and situations. He saw her die a horrible death in Hawaii, and he met her again in Athens near the Parthenon.

Louis Bromfield, in his nonfictional work *Pleasant Valley,* wrote that he had had intimations of previous lives. "France was one of the places I had always known," he declared. "From the time I was old enough to read, France had a reality for me, the one place in all the world I felt a fierce compulsion to see." He then told of his first visit there, saying, "I had seen those shores before, when I do not know"; and added that during all the years he lived there, nothing ever seemed strange to him. "It was always a country and its people whom I knew well and intimately."

Henry Ford, the automotive genius, said that he adopted the philosophy of reincarnation at the age of twenty-six, and explained, "Genius is experience. Some seem to think that it is a gift or talent, but it is the fruit of long experience in many lives. Some are older souls than others, and so they know more."

Harry Houdini, the famed magician who spent much of his life attempting to expose fraud in the mediumistic field, said in a newspaper interview that he was convinced of reincarnation. "I myself," he said, "have entered some Old World city for the first time in my life, so far as I was aware, and found the streets familiar, known just where to go to locate a certain house. Things have come to me that it seemed could only have been results of some former experience."

Congresswoman Frances P. Bolton of Ohio, in a radio interview with the late Edward R. Murrow, declared, "I believe that what we call a life-span is but one of an endless number of lifetimes during which, bit by bit, we shall experience all things."

Perhaps Arthur Schopenhauer best illustrated his belief when, a hundred years ago, he whimsically observed, "Were an Asiatic to ask me for a definition of Europe, I should be forced to answer him: It is that part of the world which is haunted by the incredible delusion that man was created out of nothing, and that his present birth is his first entrance into life."

None of this proves the cause for reincarnation, but with such an impressive panel of witnesses, we surely can afford to keep an open mind, which is the hallmark of an intelligent man.

VIII

An Eye for an Eye

THE man who is rightly credited with having done more than any other to awaken popular Western interest in reincarnation is Edgar Cayce, the late seer of Virginia Beach, who not only correctly diagnosed and prescribed treatment for the physical ailments of thousands of patients, but also gave approximately twenty-five hundred "life readings" which chronicled previous incarnations. It was Thomas Sugrue's book about Edgar Cayce, *There Is a River,* which inspired Morey Bernstein to regress a Colorado housewife to a purported previous life in Ireland, and his subsequent book, *The Search for Bridey Murphy,* became a sensation of the 1950's.

An uncommonly devout man with little formal education, Edgar Cayce had read the Bible once for each year of his life, but nothing in his religious background had prepared him for the "new" philosophy which suddenly began pouring forth while he was in a sleeplike state. The so-called "life readings" began by chance when Arthur Lammers, a prosperous Dayton printer who had become interested in metaphysics, asked Cayce for an astrological chart. In the course of supplying that information, the unconscious seer told Lammers about three of his "previous lifetimes," and said that in one of them he was a monk.

After awakening, and hearing about what he had said, the

seer was deeply disturbed. Where had such strange ideas
come from? Could this be the work of the Devil, despite
Cayce's love of God and prayers for guidance? The shaken
man walked alone all night, through the emptied streets of
Dayton, impervious to the biting cold. He had said while in
trance that the subconscious, or soul mind, is the storehouse
of all experiences and thoughts throughout our many lives.
Nothing is forgotten or lost. What could that mean?

In subsequent trance readings, Cayce helped to answer
some of his own waking questions. Why was there no mention of reincarnation in the New Testament? The sleeping
seer said that the Early Christians believed in it, and the
Gnostic sect kept alive the old "secret" teachings of early
Egyptians and Jews, but after several centuries the leaders of
the Early Church decided to drop the doctrine of reincarnation. Why? Because it made life seem complex to new converts, and because some who misinterpreted its philosophy
tended to believe that they could live as they liked, since they
would have ample opportunity to atone in future lives.

Still troubled, the seer went to his well-thumbed Bible, and
to his surprise found passages which tended to support the
theory of reincarnation. Jesus said that unless a man be born
again he cannot see the kingdom of heaven, and that unless a
man be perfect he cannot rejoin his Father. But what mere
mortal can achieve perfection in a single lifetime? In the
ninth chapter of John, when Jesus healed the man who was
blind from birth His disciples asked, "Who did sin, this man,
or his parents, that he was born blind?" How could the man
have sinned before birth, unless he had previously lived? In
the seventeenth chapter of Matthew, the disciples queried
Jesus about the Old Testament prophecy that Elias must
come before the Christ, and Jesus responded that he had
"come already, and they knew him not"; then the disciples
understood that "He spake unto them of John the Baptist."
Did this not clearly suggest that John was the reincarnation
of Elias?

Then there was the Old Testament pronouncement, "An
eye for an eye; a tooth for a tooth," and the unequivocable
statement in the thirteenth chapter of Revelations, "He that
leadeth into captivity shall go into captivity; he that killeth
with the sword must be killed with the sword." Anyone
knows that a man who kills another with a sword does not

necessarily die of a sword wound, at least in the same life-time.

As Cayce pondered these passages, he gradually came to believe that there was no more reason to doubt the legitimacy of the life readings than the physical ones. Whatever mysterious power made it possible for an uneducated man without conscious knowledge of medicine to prescribe successfully for the ailing, while in a trancelike state, also seemingly gave him access to the records of past lives. Certainly reincarnation provided a logical explanation for the obvious inequities among people he knew, some of whom were beset by so many more disabilities and problems than others.

In the trance state, Edgar Cayce was apparently able to tap cosmic consciousness, and to read the akashic records on which are supposedly written the total history of each soul from the beginning of time. Akasha is a Sanskrit word for which there is no English equivalent. It refers to the imperishable records of all thought forms and experiences in the history of mankind. Cayce, at the beginning of each life reading, enumerated significant dates and events in the current life of the subject, and the dominant character traits. These were verifiable, and not one of his clients ever disputed Cayce's accuracy in this respect. Thus, what he next stated about their previous life cycles became more believable, particularly since the episodes which he detailed tended to explain present attitudes, interests, and conduct.

Gladys Davis knew of Edgar Cayce only as her younger sister's Sunday school teacher in Selma, Alabama, when in 1923 a friend at Tissier Hardware Company asked her to take some dictation at Cayce's photographic studio. To the amazement of the eighteen-year-old stenographer, the kindly-looking gentleman seemingly went to sleep and began prescribing for the illness of her friend's afflicted nephew. Despite the unnerving conditions, Gladys made shorthand notes of the diagnosis, and as she was leaving Cayce asked for a carbon copy of her typed transcript. The seer had decided to give up photography in order to devote full time to his strange gift of clairvoyance, and a few days later he asked Gladys to go to work for him.

The psychic field sounded considerably more exciting than taking stenographic notes on nuts and bolts at the hardware company where she was then employed, but a more compelling reason influenced her decision. Musing about it after

more than forty years, Gladys says, "In that first brief encounter, I felt that I had come home. I loved my own parents, but my feeling for Mr. and Mrs. Cayce was too deep to
put into words. It was as if I belonged with them."

By the time she had given her employer a week's notice
and reported for her new duties, Cayce had gone to Dayton
with Arthur Lammers. He expected to be away only a few
days, and during his absence Mrs. Cayce read aloud each day
from her husband's previous sittings, while Gladys took them
down in shorthand, to become familiar with the odd terminology and Biblical manner of expression. Then Mrs. Cayce
and Gladys were called to Dayton, where they heard the astonishing news that the entranced seer had unexpectedly
begun to talk about reincarnation.

Reincarnation? Gladys Davis had never even heard the
word, although she vaguely recalled some mention of transmigration as a strange tenet held by many Easterners. Nothing
in her Methodist upbringing had prepared her for this belief,
but such was her faith in the Cayces that she agreed to have a
reading. The seer went into a trance, as she had seen him do
before, and soon he was telling her that because she died
from a stab wound in the breast during a Persian incarnation,
she now had a deep-seated fear of knives and cutting instruments.

The young woman was stunned by his words. Inasmuch as
Cayce barely knew her, she realized that he could not consciously have been aware of her illogical fright whenever
younger brothers held a pocket knife, or of her inner terror
when she had to peel potatoes or handle scissors. Gladys has
long since accepted the Persian experience as the root cause
of her fear, but that knowledge has failed to alleviate it, and
she still permits no sharp-pointed instruments in her kitchen,
or on her desk at Edgar Cayce headquarters.

Soon after their arrival in Dayton, Cayce's wealthy new
sponsor suffered a financial setback and they were stranded
without funds. Mrs. Cayce had brought her younger son
along, but Hugh Lynn Cayce was due to arrive shortly, and
the last of their money was used to send him train fare.
Gladys Davis could have returned home to Selma, but she
did not even consider deserting the sinking ship, although her
salary had ceased. These were her people now, and she became an integral part of the family.

Her unusual devotion to people whom she had known only

a month became more understandable, when in a subsequent reading she heard that in prehistoric Egypt she had been the daughter of Edgar Cayce, who was then the high priest Rata, and of Gertrude Cayce, then a beautiful priestess. The reading stated that Gladys' earthly sojourn in that lifetime was fleeting. She died of grief at the age of four, after her parents were exiled and forced to leave her behind with the king. Still later, Gladys learned that she and the Cayces were members of a close-knit family group in a Persian incarnation, but in a different relationship; and that groups of souls tend to return at approximately the same time, into situations which can again bring them together.

In her first life reading, Cayce had described Gladys as "one whose greatest force will lie in the home and the dedication of its better self to future generations of its own strain." She assumed that he meant she would have numerous children, but she did not marry until the age of forty-six, after both Gertrude and Edgar Cayce were dead. Even as a teenager, however, Gladys had wished for a son. Not for a husband or daughter, but a son. Several years after she went to live with the Cayces, a younger brother's marriage failed, and for a time she was permitted to have his baby boy with her. Throughout the years since, a mother-son relationship has endured between them, and the little son of the now-grown nephew calls Gladys "Granny."

A Cayce reading helped to explain her lifelong yearning for a son, in these terms: As a French matron during the reign of Louis XIV, she grieved so deeply over the death of her three-year-old son that she entered a Catholic convent, but remained inconsolable and soon died. This deep understanding of bereavement may have influenced her choice of parents in the present incarnation, since her mother lost her only child nine months before Gladys Davis was born.

Hugh Lynn Cayce was sixteen years old when his father's apparent ability to delve into past lives was discovered. It was a month before the lad heard about this strange turn of events, and after joining the family in Dayton he was as shocked as Edgar Cayce had been, on learning about his trance discussion of reincarnation. A reading on Hugh Lynn had been given before his arrival, since the seer did not need for the person to be present, and among the odd events described was this:

During a prehistoric Egyptian incarnation Hugh Lynn's

brother had stolen his wife, precipitating a tribal war; but after Hugh Lynn resoundingly defeated him, he generously permitted the brother to keep the woman because they were in love. The elder Cayce added cryptically that Hugh Lynn had again known the woman in an English lifetime, but supplied no further details. Sometime later, one of Hugh Lynn's school friends in Dayton requested a Cayce reading, and heard that he had been the brother in that long-ago Egyptian lifetime.

The Cayces subsequently moved to Virginia Beach, and Hugh Lynn fell in love with an attractive girl from Minneapolis, whose family was vacationing at the beach. He gave her his fraternity pin, and after they had been engaged for two years, he asked his father to give a life reading for her. In it, she was identified as the wife who had been stolen by his brother during the Egyptian incarnation. Intrigued by the odd chain of circumstances which had again attracted him to the unfaithful wife and brother, Hugh Lynn decided that it would be interesting to see how they reacted to each other in this lifetime. He said nothing to either about the other, but since his fiancée and her parents were again coming to the beach for a visit, he invited his Dayton friend at the same time.

During the week's visit, Hugh Lynn could observe no spark of emotion between them; and after his fiancée returned to Minneapolis, the Ohio friend exclaimed, "That's the worst one you've ever found. I didn't like her at all." He remained for several more days, and then borrowed money from Hugh Lynn to pay his train fare home. A week later, Hugh Lynn's fiancée mailed back his fraternity pin, explaining that his friend had followed her to Minneapolis. Apparently deciding that confession was good for the soul, she added that during the week at Virginia Beach they had "borrowed" Hugh Lynn's car for late dates, after he went to bed, and were "madly in love."

The couple's torrid romance soon ended, but so had their friendship with Hugh Lynn, who later was happily married to a Virginia Beach girl. In 1944, now the father of a baby son, he was drafted into the army, and while stationed at Fort Meade, Maryland, he accidentally swallowed a plum pit which nearly strangled him before an emergency operation could be performed. He recovered and shipped overseas with a Special Services outfit, but while in England suffered another choking spell when a piece of gristle lodged in his throat. Thereafter he had repeated recurrences of the trouble, and twice had to be hospitalized.

After the war Hugh Lynn returned to Virginia Beach, but while celebrating the homecoming with his wife and friends he again choked violently, and was in such critical condition that nurses had to strap his hands and feet to the operating table, as a surgeon fought against time to remove a chicken-bone from his windpipe. Three days later he received a letter from a California acquaintance, who was puzzled by a dream which occurred the night of Hugh Lynn's operation, although he had no knowledge of that event. He wrote that he saw a desperately heaving man whose hands and feet were strapped to a board. That much paralleled the hospital experience, and could have been written down as clairvoyance; but the man in the dream was being tortured on a medieval rack for some dire misdeed, and as the slumbering friend moved closer, he recognized the man as Hugh Lynn, "despite the long, yellow, dirty hair."

That night Hugh Lynn had one of the most vivid dreams of his life. Its setting was a rough hovel in England at the time of the Norse invasions. His yellow hair was scraggly and unkempt, and he burned with murderous rage as he choked a woman who was refusing to identify the man responsible for her pregnancy. Then, as if a television camera had panned in for a close-up, he recognized her as his former fiancée from Minneapolis. Now he seemed to be living both experiences simultaneously, in a kind of double consciousness. He was keenly aware of her repeated infidelity, but as he strangled her, his violent anger suddenly subsided and he began desperately entreating God to forgive the philandering woman, the unfaithful friend, and himself.

So intense were his prayers that they awakened him, and with a deep sense of horror he "knew" that he had been re-living a macabre soul memory. With that realization came an outpouring of thanksgiving that the Dayton friend had spared him a third marital disaster with the same woman, and he earnestly sought forgiveness for his own foul deed. The next day, summoned to the telephone, he heard the voice of the former sweetheart whom he had not seen since that long-ago parting at the beach. She said that the cruise ship on which she was sailing for South America had stopped at Norfolk for repairs, and she wanted to ask if Hugh Lynn could ever

forgive her for what she had done. She must have been startled by the unusual fervor with which he assured her that he
had already done so; and in the more than two decades since,
he has had no further choking bouts.

Hugh Lynn's wartime service seems also to have triggered
another soul memory. His life readings had said that he partic-
ipated in the Crusades, but the elder Cayce indicated that
boredom with medieval village life rather than spiritual zeal
had been his motivation. The day that World War II ended,
Hugh Lynn was stationed in an Austrian village near the Ba-
varian border. Allied troops had "liberated" some Austrian
beer, and he was enjoying a canteen cup of it while sitting in
the yard of a neat little cottage, when his mind began to play
tricks on him.

"The main road through the village was crowded," he recalls. "Remnants of the Austrian army, bedraggled, dirty,
thin and exhausted, plodded by. American trucks raced back
and forth, picking up airplane parts which were cached at intervals along the roadside. Prisoners from a nearby work
camp had been released, and the Poles, Russians and Czechs
were rushing down the road as if they would run all the way
to their homes in eastern Europe. Imprisoned for years, now
free, these men were singing and laughing hysterically, as
were captured British airmen who were headed for the air-
fields to be flown home. Excitement, relief, joy and fear
blended into an emotional wave which seemed almost tangi-
ble."

Hugh Lynn recalls that as he surveyed the confusion,
"something clicked in my head and I saw before me a marching horde of Crusaders; men in armor on horses, men dressed
in leather carrying spears, servants walking alongside, some
with leather coverings on their arms on which hooded falcons
perched. Little dwarfs acted as entertainers, tumbling along at
the side of the marching column. It seemed that I was literally back in the time of the Crusades."

As abruptly as the vision came, it vanished. Then came a
strange awareness of the little Austrian village. Hugh Lynn
knew where he could find the ruin of an old building whose
stones had later been used for village structures. He knew
where there would be a stone bridge over a small stream.
With that awareness came the sense that he had once lived
just around the corner, and that when marching Crusaders
reached his village he had deserted a wife and small child to

seek adventure with them. The next day, without benefit of beer, he easily located what appeared to be the ruins of the old building and the bridge, precisely where he knew that they would be.

"The war began and ended for me in that little Austrian village," he says thoughtfully. "In that much earlier war to liberate Jerusalem, I had deliberately walked away from family responsibilities. In this war, I was drafted; forced to leave my wife, young son, and parents, with whom I longed to be. Both my father and mother had died while I was away."

Perhaps this was a circle come full turn, which settled for Hugh Lynn Cayce another karmic debt.

Not all of Hugh Lynn's soul memories have been prompted by his father's life readings for him. As a youngster in Selma, Alabama, he avidly devoured every book in the library on Daniel Boone and the early settlement of Kentucky. "It was like eating peanuts," he says ruefully.

He had never been a Boy Scout, but as an adult in Virginia Beach he became a Scoutmaster, and discovered that he knew precisely how to select the proper hardwood to build small fires which never smoked, even when he cooked over them. The day that he stepped into his first canoe, he paddled it as expertly as a frontiersman. He devised games for the Scout troops, to teach them how to stalk, track, and disguise trails, and thought that they were original, until he later learned that they were old Indian games. Fishing, hunting, and pitching tents came as naturally to him as eating, and as a small boy he had constructed adult-sized bows and arrows without instruction.

"Could it be," he wonders, "that I once played with Indians in early Kentucky days, that my life in that incarnation was cut short, and that as a consequence my interests then became my hobbies today?"

Petite, glamorous Lucille Kahn was playing on Broadway with Lionel Barrymore in David Belasco's production of *Laugh Clown Laugh*, when she met David Kahn, a World War I army captain who happened to share her surname. After he joined her court of admirers, Lucille laughingly told other members of the cast, "David tells the most fascinating stories I've ever heard, but I don't believe a one of them. They're all kookie."

The stories that she found so amusing concerned Edgar

Cayce, whom David and his family had met in their home-
town of Lexington, Kentucky, long before the seer achieved
national fame. In 1910, Cayce gave a physical reading for
David's ailing brother, Leon, and his mother was so impressed by Cayce's remarkable powers that she told her eldest
son, "David, I want you to promise that you will devote a
portion of your life to seeing that the work of this man is
made known to the world. The world needs him." David sol-
emnly promised, and during his war service overseas he frequently spoke of Cayce to his buddies. After his return to civilian life, he went to visit Cayce, and became an active sponsor of his work.

Lucille, the daughter of a French-born mother and of a
language professor from Alsace-Lorraine, was born in Okla-
homa, where her parents had set up housekeeping after their
marriage in Texas. At an early age, the little girl showed such
aptitude for the violin that her parents sent her to the Kidd-
Key Conservatory in Texas, and later to Chicago Musical
College for advanced study. Although her teachers considered
Lucilla a virtuoso, she felt keen dissatisfaction with her own
performance, sensing that her execution of the compositions
did not measure up to the music that she heard within.

She longed to be an actress, but knowing that her parents
would disapprove, she enrolled secretly in a dramatic arts
class offered by the college. There she at last found the inner
satisfaction that had eluded her, and evinced such talent that
when the director of a touring stock company asked the head
of the drama department to recommend an ingenue, he
promptly suggested Lucille Kahn. Through the intercession of
a family friend, the reluctant approval of her parents was obtained, and within three years she was appearing at the Belasco Theater on Broadway.

In 1924 she was cast in the feminine lead, opposite Otis
Skinner, in *Sancho Panza*, and as they prepared to take the
show on the road, David Kahn begged Lucille to see Edgar
Cayce when the company reached Dayton, Ohio. Only because of his persistence, Lucille sent word that complimen-
tary tickets would be awaiting the Cayces at the box office
for the evening performance, and that she would like to call
on them the next morning.

Recalling the circumstances more than four decades later,
Lucille says, "When I presented myself at their home that
morning, Mr. Cayce was preparing to give a trance reading

in absentia for a dying child, and I was allowed to sit in on it. I was never so shocked in my life! In fact, I was outraged. Here was a child whom even the doctors could not help, and this semiliterate man was instructing the parents to put it on an all-banana diet. I thought that Edgar Cayce should be locked up! How could I know that before long, a banana diet would become standard medical treatment for that particular ailment?"

At David's urging, Lucille dutifully requested a life reading, and she was reluctantly forced to concede that at least some of it seemed to ring true. The seer told her that in a previous lifetime she had resided in the home of a German composer, where she learned to understand, but not play music. "The urge in the present is the ear or innate feeling of music, rather than the free expression of same," the reading declared. "Not that the entity is not a musician, but feels it rather than acts it." Lucille realized that Cayce had no conscious way of knowing that she had once been an aspiring musician, since she had seen no reason to mention it even to David, and she says of it, "I must admit that I was deeply impressed by so subtle an observation. No one had ever known my inner despair or doubts concerning a career in music—so gnawing that I was blindly compelled to follow my great longing to be in the theater."

The reading further stated that in several previous incarnations she had been in the theater. "We find in the days of Pliny in the Grecian country, the entity was then in the name Poyane and of beautiful figure and stature, giving much to the peoples in the way of the Arts and acting. Under the influence of Tacitus the entity gained much favor from many peoples. This, in a portion of the life, proved detrimental to the entity. The love of stage and applause is innate from this appearance in the earth's plane. Well that some of this be kept under control of will."

Despite the odd terminology, Lucille realized that Cayce was warning her against delight in applause and attention; and although she did not then believe in reincarnation, she knew that she was what people colloquially called "a natural-born actress." From the very beginning of her stage career she had required little direction, and she remembered that Plato had said, "New knowledge, easily gained, is old knowledge." It had to come from somewhere within her, she supposed, and none of her known ancestors had ever been interested in the stage.

The reading indicated that Lucille could achieve considerable success either as an actress or a wife, but not in both pursuits; and that her greatest spiritual unfoldment occurred during a life in India when she had helped to correlate religious teachings from Egypt as well as India, to disseminate to the people.

Lucille frankly acknowledges that she loves the excitement of the spotlight and the sound of applause, but three years after the reading she gave up the theater to marry David Kahn. Shortly thereafter, the young couple paid a visit to the Cayces, who by then were living in Virginia Beach, and for the first time Lucille met Hugh Lynn and his good friend Thomas Sugrue. Their youthful enthusiasm for Cayce's work was contagious, and after catching their excitement about a world beyond our five senses, she became an omnivorous reader of Eastern philosophy having to do with reincarnation and karma.

In New York she met such luminaries as Gerald Heard and Aldous Huxley, who steered her to the Tibetan Book of the Dead and other psychic works. She became an active sponsor of Sugrue's lectures on metaphysics, and after his death was asked to take over the lecture series. Mindful of the warning that she should not seek applause in this lifetime, Lucille rejected the spotlighted role for herself, but agreed to launch a yearly subscription series which featured world-famous lecturers on extrasensory perception, together with highly respected philosophers, psychiatrists, psychologists and medical doctors who had delved into the psychic. So successful was the project that it still continues to attract leading lecturers in the field, and a cross section of New York society. Thus, the work of correlating religious beliefs and philosophies, which reportedly occupied her talents thousands of years ago in India, has again become her abiding interest, and she is now chairman of the board of the Association for Research and Enlightenment, which carries on Cayce's work.

Shortly after the Kahns were married, the widowed secretary of an officer of General Electric Corporation consulted them about her problems in rearing a five-year-old son whose father had recently died. David requested a Cayce reading for the child, and it said that on the basis of a past incarnation he could become a leader in the architectural field, particularly as related to city planning. As the years passed, the boy evinced no interest whatsoever in architecture or building. He chose an arts and science course at Yale University, and upon graduation went into the army. During the postwar occupation of Japan, however, he was placed in charge of billeting American soldiers and overseeing the conversion of Japanese barracks to American requirements. This work entailed supervising the building of new compounds, and he became so interested in housing that on returning to civilian life he enrolled at Massachusetts Institute of Technology for post-graduate work in architecture.

He chose for his master's thesis a city planning project which involved the conversion from streetcars to buses, the relocation of terminals, rerouting of streets and construction of buildings. His thesis was considered so outstanding that his professor recommended him to a leading firm in city planning, where he is now a partner. He also edits a national magazine in the field, and has served as president of the American Society for City Planning.

This prominent architect insists that rather than having been drawn to the field because of the suggestion contained in the Cayce reading, he actively resisted it, but that a "compelling force within" eventually pushed him into a career for which he had apparently developed talent in a previous lifetime.

IX

Group Karma

EDGAR CAYCE gave a number of life readings himself, and never ceased to be surprised by the material which came forth. As these readings progressed, he discovered that he had been a member of five different racial groups and religions, during his many lifetimes dating back to prehistoric Egyptian times; and that many of those who surrounded him in this life had been relatives, friends, associates, or unfriendly rivals in ages past. The readings stressed that groups of souls tend to reincarnate together in cycles, meeting each other again and again in earthly lives, and being drawn together by some curious law of karmic attraction in order to work out mutual problems which had been left unresolved. Cayce further said that souls change sex as well as nationality and race, from time to time, depending on what role can best serve the purpose for which they chose to be reborn.

An abrupt shift to the opposite gender after several incarnations as a man, or as a woman, could provide a clue to the problem of homosexuality. A person so afflicted may be subconsciously pining for the physique with which he was more familiar, but by understanding that he selected the new role in order to balance his spiritual growth, he could more easily free himself of karmic fetters that are retarding his normal development.

In his waking state Edgar Cayce was a humble, devoted family man who regularly taught a Presbyterian Sunday school class until his death in 1945. Upon going into self-induced trance, however, he seemed to see another dimension and meaning of life. He learned that as a high priest in ancient Egypt he had acquired, through many disciplines, a higher state of consciousness than those around him. As an Arabian desert chieftain in a subsequent incarnation he had suffered such physical torture, when left to die in the hot sands, that he had managed temporarily to release his consciousness from his body to escape the agony. This faculty, which made it possible for him to survive, was also used to aid others; and because nothing is ever lost or forgotten by the subconscious, he was able to tap this inner resource during the incarnation as Edgar Cayce.

He had become a physician in the Persian lifetime, and had established a healing center in "the city in the hills and the plains," where patients could be treated through diet, massage, therapy and steam baths, and with herbal medicines. Thus, he was seemingly able to draw upon this latent knowledge in twentieth-century America, prescribing for thousands of others while in trance, and also healing himself of such ailments as paralysis of the vocal cords, pneumonia, and a severe blow on the head. Cayce had earned the right to this inner knowledge through self-imposed disciplines, and although the readings indicated that he was by no means as saintly in some of his incarnations as in others, certainly during the lifetime as Edgar Cayce he used his remarkable talents only in a spirit of helpfulness, and accomplished great good.

The seer's ever-growing reputation rests almost entirely on the physical and life readings which he gave while in trance, but his psychic attunement was such that even in the conscious state he came to "recognize" many strangers as entites whom he had known in past lives. As his fame grew, hundreds of these people flocked to Virginia Beach to meet the remarkable man about whom they had read, only to learn in subsequent readings that they had "known" him centuries before.

This would seem to bear out the assertions of Dr. Rudolf Steiner and other famous nineteenth-century psychics, as well as Cayce, that groups of souls between lives reach some kind of agreement on when to take up earthly lives again. Thus, we would never know in the physical plane some of the entities who were returning in a different cycle than our own, but might often encounter them in the spiritual realm.

The seeming tendency for certain souls to be drawn closely together, time and again in earthly situations, is called group karma, and the most effective way to illustrate it is to cite the case of a close-knit, but often antagonistic family, all of whose members were said to have known each other in varying relationships during several previous incarnations. Edgar Cayce repeatedly stressed that unless we are willing to be linked, in lifetime after lifetime, with a person whom we dislike, we would be well advised to begin working now at dissolving the animosity which forges that bond.

Almost every visitor to the headquarters of the Association for Research and Enlightenment at Virginia Beach is struck by the poise and serenity of Mae Gimbert St. Clair, the attractive researcher and receptionist who is ordinarily the first person he meets. I say "almost" any visitor, because more than two decades ago, a New York woman who had intended to remain for two weeks departed in a huff the following morning, because she felt such antagonism for Mrs. St. Clair. But more of that later.

Mae Gimbert was one of six children born to a farmer and his wife in Oceana, Virginia, a rural area which is now only ten minutes via superhighway from Norfolk, but was then a half day's journey by meandering dirt roads from the bright lights of the city. For plumbing the Gimberts had an outhouse and a well. Churning butter was a daily routine. The children attended a consolidated country school, and their social life revolved around the church. It was a page from primitive Americana, in the heart of twentieth-century Tidewater Virginia.

In her sixth grade at school, Mae felt romantically attracted to a boy four years her senior, many of whose classmates behaved toward him like a retinue of loyal courtesans. It was several years before he deigned to take note of the worshipful young girl, but at the age of seventeen Mae eloped with him, despite the outspoken disapproval of her family. The young couple moved in with his socialite family, which was considerably more worldly than Mae's; and she says in retrospect, "It was like stepping from Fort Dearborn into the glittering, dissolute court of Louis XIV." The significance of this remark will soon become apparent.

Within six months after her marriage, the unsophisticated bride discovered that her charming, debonair husband was drinking and enjoying the company of other women. Some nights he did not even bother to come home, and she could find no solace, because his parents apparently condoned his behavior. Because her own family had sought to prevent the marriage, Mae was reluctant to take her heartache to them, so she often poured out her troubles to a kindly neighbor woman. By this time, she and her husband had moved to a rented house at Virginia Beach, and Mae occasionally stopped in at a hamburger stand owned by Boyd Davis, who once asked her if she had heard of Edgar Cayce. When she replied in the negative, he told her a little about the famous seer for whom his sister Gladys worked, and suggested that she drop in at the new Cayce hospital that Sunday to hear his lecture on reincarnation. Mae, assuming that this was the same as transmigration of souls into animals, gave the conversation no further thought. Who needed reincarnation? She had troubles enough as it was.

Mae lived with an aching heart for nearly five years, before finally leaving the husband whom she still loved. She went to New York, where her older sister was working on a master's degree at Columbia University. Mae had to get a job, but without experience the only work she could find was waiting on tables at a restaurant in the Wall Street area. One day, two of her customers asked where she was from, and when she replied that her home was Virginia Beach, David Kahn said he supposed that she knew Edgar Cayce. On learning that she did not, he gave her a letter of introduction and urged, "You ought to get a reading from him. A girl with your obvious breeding has no business working as a waitress. He could tell you what you ought to do with your life."

Mae was so discouraged that on her next visit home she told her mother about the conversation, and then went to see Edgar Cayce; but on learning that the fee for a reading was twenty dollars, she did not pursue it. In her financial state since the divorce, twenty dollars might as well have been twenty thousand. Among other frequenters of the Wall Street restaurant was a young man who annoyed Mae by continually asking her for dates. He had made a bet that he could get a date with the pretty, standoffish waitress who refused to go out with customers, but she was then unaware of this; and he proved so persistent that she finally agreed, on one condition: that he take her to the rodeo at Madison Square Garden. The young statistician was willing to go anyplace in order to win his wager with the boys, so he took her there by taxi, all the way from Wall Street. Afterward, he escorted her to a famous restaurant, but she passed up the tempting delectables in favor of a liverwurst sandwich. She was not interested in spending his money; just in seeing the horses perform at the rodeo.

Mae did not particularly enjoy John's company, but she kept thinking how "right" he seemed for the sister with whom she was living; so when he asked her for a second date, she consented in order that the two of them could meet. John called for her at the apartment, but she had barely completed the introductions when her sister flounced haughtily from the room. Thereafter, the sister studiously avoided meeting John, even when Mae, frightened because she herself seemed to have become emotionally dead inside, finally accepted his marriage proposal.

They moved to Virginia Beach, but with the depression now in full swing, the only work that John could locate in his line was a night job. He was violently jealous of anyone whom Mae had previously known; so, although her first husband was no longer in the area, she cut herself off from their mutual friends and spent long winter evenings alone, often wrapped in quilts to keep warm, because they could afford only enough heat to prevent the water pipes in the house from freezing. It soon became apparent that the marriage was not going well. John seemed to distrust her every move, and the harder she tried, the less she could please him.

One evening, almost overcome with depression, Mae persuaded John to drop her off at the home of a friend, on his way to work. It was the woman who had given her such a sympathetic ear when her first marriage was breaking up, and she had not seen her since, but the friend was the gregarious type who always welcomed callers unannounced. As fate would have it, Boyd and Burlynn Davis also happened to drop in that evening, although they had also been out of contact with the mutual friend for several years.

All of them greeted Mae with warm affection, and when the Davis couple invited her to their new restaurant the following evening, the lonely girl was only too happy to accept. Now, all of the karmic blocks were beginning to move into place, although Mae had no way of knowing it. The evening started off happily enough, but with the suddenness of a thunderbolt Mae became acutely ill, and recognized the unmistakable symptoms of a physical condition for which she had twice previously undergone painful, expensive operations. She burst into tears, and desperately told her hosts, "I give up! My emotions have been drained, and I'll never find happiness. Now I'll have to be operated on again, because it's the only way there is to treat this condition. I simply can't go on! I don't want to live. I want to die!"

While Burlynn tried to make Mae physically comfortable, Boyd Davis pleaded with her to have a physical reading with Edgar Cayce. Looking back on that fateful time, May says, "I didn't even have the price of a Coke, let alone twenty dollars, but Boyd was so sure I could be cured through a reading that he said he would pay Mr. Cayce himself, if I had to have an operation. What did I have to lose? I was too emotionally spent to care, but before going to Mr. Cayce I first talked it over with my family. We were always tremendously involved with each other—willful and determined and argumentative —all except my wonderful mother, who was 'loaned' to us in this lifetime. I told them I was going to have a reading with Mr. Cayce, and if they had any objections to speak up now, because whatever he prescribed I intended to do. They were violently opposed to 'fortune-telling,' but they knew I was facing another dangerous operation and was highly unstrung, so for once in their lives they did not try to block me."

Mae says that when she arrived at the Cayces' she was "nervous, confused, fearful, and utterly self-centered," but that after Cayce began to speak, "it was as if a ton of crushing stones had been removed from my head and body." The reading prescribed a course of treatments and emphasized the need for continual warmth. Inasmuch as the temperature of her own house was barely above freezing, and the treatments could not be self-administered, Boyd and Burlynn Davis took her into their home to nurse her. Within ten days she was well, and has since had no recurrence of the trouble.

Overjoyed at her healing, Mae often dropped in to see the Cayces, and the seer began asking when she was going to have a life reading. Each time, she replied that she would not do so until she had erased her financial indebtedness to him, which she was paying off at the rate of a dollar a month. Finally, he said that he would give her one anyway, and on the day in 1938 that she sat in his study, while he again went into trance, a whole new vista opened for her.

The reading said that in an incarnation late in the eighteenth century she was married to a tavern keeper at Fort Dearborn, on the present site of Chicago, and that like most feminine habitués of the combination dance hall and gambling parlor, she was a woman of easy virtue. It identified one of her brothers today as her husband then, a second brother as one of the boys at the bar in the tavern, and a third brother as a brother also in that lifetime. Her present father was the sheriff at Fort Dearborn, her present mother was her confidante and landlady, and a sister-in-law and various other relatives were also known to her then in varying relationships.

The reading further declared that she was a good friend of John Bainbridge, a shrewd gambler who frequented the tavern; and that when Fort Dearborn burned to the ground during the French and Indian Wars, Bainbridge helped many of the inhabitants to escape, but drowned while saving Mae's life in a river crossing. What Mae did not then realize was that Cayce had previously identified himself in a trance reading as Bainbridge, and that he had "recognized her soul" when Mae came for the physical reading.

In the latter part of that lifetime, Mae reportedly amassed considerable good karma to balance the bad that she had earlier acquired. The reading stated that those who escaped from Fort Dearborn scattered to various parts of the country, and that Mae joined a group which came to Tidewater, Virginia. She had lost her husband, child, and worldly goods, but she eventually opened a boardinghouse; and during the War of 1812 she nursed back to health anyone who came to her door for help, becoming known as "The Angel."

Mae had been a skeptic who laughed at Boyd Davis's belief in reincarnation, but one reason why the life reading made sense to her was because the sleeping seer had begun it by accurately pinpointing events which had already transpired in her present life, saying, "Nineteen thirty-five, a change; nineteen twenty-eight, what a period of turmoil!" It was in 1928 that Mae, desperate about the behavior of her husband and his family, finally put her foot down and demanded that he find them a house of their own at Virginia Beach; and in 1935 she married again. Thus, she listened intently as Cayce described still another of her alleged incarnations, in France, when she was said to have been a lady-in-waiting who caught the roving eye of Louis XIV, and became one of his consorts. At that time, according to the reading, she was the same age as when she eloped in this lifetime. Soon, however, the king replaced her with a new favorite, and after she had resentfully tried in every way to undermine the court, she finally became a nun.

The king, his ego somewhat deflated by her desertion, demanded that she renounce her vow, and only with the strong backing of the Church was she able to withstand the very real temptation to do so. Years later, Mae was to discover that a very similar romance had actually occurred, and that Alexander Dumas had already written a fictionalized account of the affair which was recited that day to her by a semiliterate seer, who could not have heard of it by ordinary means.

What really made everything seem to fall into place for Mae, however, was Cayce's assertion that her first husband was a reincarnation of Louis XIV. From Fort Dearborn to the dissolute court of seventeenth-century France! She had begun her present life in conditions nearly as primitive as those in that little frontier trading post on Lake Michigan, where she had known and loved horses. Could that explain why she gave a date to John, only on condition that she could see the horse show at Madison Square Garden? Certainly, the reading suggested why she had felt such irresistible attraction toward the first husband, defying her own family to take on the more sophisticated trappings of his life, and forlornly holding onto him for such a long time after he became interested in other women.

The Cayce reading said that Mae's second husband, John, was married to her present sister during the Fort Dearborn incarnation, and that after Mae nursed him back to health in Tidewater, his wife accused her of stealing him; "and the jealousy turned to suspicion and then to hate." Mae says that this also seemed credible, "because my sister and I have been warring since I was knee-high," and it could also have accounted for the sister's peculiar attitude toward John, when Mae tried to bring the two of them together. One of the best-documented cases in the files at the Association for Research and Enlightenment headquarters is the series of physical readings which Cayce subsequently gave for Mae's sister, who spent five years in a tuberculosis sanitarium before she could be persuaded to consult the seer. Numerous X rays

taken before and after indicate that by following his prescribed treatments, she was cured in less than three years, and
in the three decades since has had no recurrence of TB.

Edgar Cayce told Mae of other lifetimes in Palestine,
Egypt and Atlantis, and detailed her association with members of her present family in each of them. He said that in
Palestine she had converted the man who was her second
husband in this lifetime, but that in the French incarnation
she had used him to "get back at" Louis XIV, which could
have explained his jealousy and mistrust of Mae in the present.

Musing about the regularity with which she has apparently
reencountered members of her present family, Mae says, "But
it was in the Fort Dearborn incarnation that we became
members of a close-knit group, and it is in our present life
that we have finally had to face our karmic relationships,
both good and bad, as a family unit; for Mr. Cayce made
clear that enemies as well as friends from past lives can
choose to share a household situation in order to work out
karmic problems."

Mae's reading said that in Palestine, as a member of a
Greco-Roman family, she was called Vesta; that she was associated with some of the disciples and became a deaconess
in the Early Church. It further stated that she was married
and had three children, but that her husband left her for a
younger woman; and several years after the reading, Mae
met her rival of that lifetime. It was the woman from New
York who, although she had no idea of Mae's identity in a
previous incarnation, had felt such instantaneous animosity
toward her that she canceled her reservations for a two-week
stay. Mae says that she had also felt strangely excitable
around the woman, although not until she discussed it with
Mr. Cayce did she understand why.

That same life reading in 1938 told Mae that she would
face another change in 1941, and early in 1941 her first husband returned to Virginia Beach after a long absence. To her
dismay, Mae kept encountering him on the streets, and although she repeatedly declined his invitations to join him for
a drink, she became so agitated that she went to Edgar Cayce
for advice. The seer gave her another reading, during which
he counseled in so many words, "You've been through this
before, in a previous lifetime with him. Don't let it happen
again."

Mae says of this emotional upheaval, "I could feel the old flame flaring whenever I chanced to see him. I yearned to go back to him, just as I had in the French incarnation. The Church had served as my buffer in that lifetime, and Mr. Cayce in this one; for Mr. Cayce made me see that the reason I had had to repeat my error now was because nearly three hundred years ago, although I had physically separated myself from the king, my mental and emotional longing for him had prolonged the unfortunate entanglement. Mr. Cayce made me realize that unless I healed myself of this infatuation now, it would lead to a continuation of a karmic tie that was far better dissolved."

The first husband, apparently in the hope of seeing Mae, made an appointment for a Cayce reading, which revealed, among other things, a serious physical ailment for which treatments were prescribed, but he failed to follow them. Mae, realizing that the man also needed to rid himself of the karmic fetter that tied him to her, occasionally talked to him, and tried to persuade him to follow the Cayce course of treatments, but it was of no avail. At last, realizing that their ideals were so diametrically opposed that any further contact was useless, Mae was able to free her heart of his pull on its strings.

In a voice tinged with awe, Mae says of her hardships in this lifetime, "But look at this Universal Law at work! How did it happen that after all those years, I chose that particular evening to go to see the woman who had befriended me during my first marital disaster? And how did Boyd and Burlynn happen to drop in on her that evening, after a long absence? What if I had not been visiting the Davises the next evening, when I became so ill! Because of that, I met Mr. Cayce, and he not only changed my life but that of my entire family. He seemed to feel that this was his opportunity to right the karmic wrongs of his own loose living in the Fort Dearborn period, when so many of us had been a close-knit group. There is little question but that his physical readings for my parents prolonged their lives by twenty years, and that the treatments prescribed for my sister, two nieces, a nephew, a cousin, an aunt and other relatives also effected cures for them. He gave me work when I was desperately in need; but more importantly, he gave meaning and purpose to my

speak with this composed, charming woman today, it is

almost impossible to visualize the frightened, emotionally drained young matron who had desperately wanted to die. She is now a widow, and during the many years that she has devoted herself to the Edgar Cayce Foundation, she has found an inner serentity which more than compensates for the hard knocks of this lifetime. Surely she will have earned an easier niche the next time around!

X

Keeper of the Records

BEVERLY SIMMONS had the unique experience of being told by Edgar Cayce that she was the reincarnation of his older sister, who died shortly before his own birth in Kentucky. The wife of Riley Simmons, a prominent Norfolk insurance executive, had heard for several years about "the strange goings-on" in nearby Virginia Beach before her curiosity finally prompted her to request a Cayce reading. She attended the sitting in November of 1940, and listened with mounting interest as the seer precisely pinpointed her character traits.

He said that she was outwardly serene but deeply emotional within, having a tendency for sudden changes of mood; that she was "free from needs of companionship," and had an "intense need" for frequent intervals of solitude, at which time she had an odd habit of humming under her breath. She could not have described herself more accurately. He further said that she sometimes felt a "necessity" for lots of bangling jewelry, while at other times she scorned to wear any, and tended to take a what's-the-use attitude toward life. He added that she had great ability with facts and figures (she has held a highly responsible position as a bookkeeper for many years), and a rare capacity for making a success of marriage and a career simultaneously.

The unconscious seer had been dissecting her character as

neatly as a surgeon, when he suddenly startled her by declaring, "Before this, the entity as Leila Cayce entered the earthly experience for a period that brought hope, then sorrow, to many." He said that after failing to find the environment that she had expected, she withdrew from this life at the age of two years and eight months. Referring to the akashic source of his out-of-this-world knowledge, Cayce continued, "Yes, we are given the records here of that entity known as Leila Cayce . . . Leila Beverly Cayce."

"At mention of the middle name of the sister he had never known, even Cayce's longtime secretary, Gladys Davis, started with surprise. It seemed an eerie coincidence that in this lifetime the name Beverly should also have been bestowed by a different set of parents, and Mrs. Simmons later learned from her mother that except for her father's objections she would have been named Lyal Beverly, an even closer approximation of Leila Beverly.

Another coincidence came to light as Cayce continued: "The entity Leila Beverly Cayce departed [this life] on the twenty-fourth of August, 1876. It entered again on the twenty-fourth of August, 1910," on the thirty-fourth anniversary of the "death." The seer said that Leila Cayce was born to two very differently tempered individuals, and that "an activity upon the part of the earthly father brought that disappointment which caused the entity to seek deeper meditation." In other words, to die. He explained that for the first two or three years, a soul is given the right to withdraw if a parent has induced unanticipated changes, which Leila's father did. He said the child also intuitively realized that she had selected an environment in which it would not be possible for her to meet the husband of several previous incarnations.

Later, when Cayce's words were read back to him, he recalled his mother having said that ten days after Leila's birth, her husband went on an extended bout with the bottle, and that thereafter the baby seemed to waste away until it died. Curiously, when Leila reportedly reincarnated as Beverly, precisely thirty-four years later, the present father was also a heavy drinker, and she had such a strong aversion to liquor that she refused to date boys who drank. Thus, she seemingly chose to return to the same problem in order to meet it more courageously.

The unconscious Cayce told Mrs. Simmons that she almost

withdrew from her present body at exactly the same age as before, and although her mother does not believe in reincarnation, she subsequently confirmed that a few months before Beverly's third birthday, the child seemed so near death from no known cause that she had her picture taken, as a keepsake.

Pictures of Beverly Simmons as an adult are also of considerable interest, for when compared with photographs of Edgar Cayce's youngest sister, Sarah Cayce Hesson, the family resemblance is so marked that the two women could almost have been doubles.

One of the most unusual remarks ever made by the highly unusual Edgar Cayce was volunteered as he emerged from the trance reading on Beverly as Leila. "It is the only time," he said, "I've had the Keeper of Records point out to me what I can read. Always before he has merely handed me the book, but here he guided my reading of the book and pointed with his finger at the passages I might read, and told me what parts to skip until later." Mrs. Simmons is of the opinion that futher details might have been too painful for the Cayce family.

Another Cayce reading acquainted Mrs. Simmons with an excitingly different existence in seventeenth-century England as Marge Oglethorpe, who was said to be the daughter of Governor J. B. Oglethorpe, the founder of Georgia, although apparently an illegitimate offspring. The sleeping Cayce always couched his phraseology in tactful terms, but it is obvious from the reading that the beautiful belle who reportedly cut a wide swath in British social circles was headstrong, willful, imperious, and naughty. She was "not a snob," but one who honestly considered herself "a little bit better than anyone else," he said, and a feeling of superiority "must be guarded against" in this lifetime. The reading declared that Marge Oglethorpe brought "turmoils" to others by her seeking for "pomp and favor," and added, "As to the social activities and some of these escapades that were not pretty, these we would pass since they have little to do with the present experience of the entity." The pleasure-seeking girl must eventually have mended her ways, because Cayce saw her in later years kneeling before a convent altar, but he said that records of "that wayward Oglethorpe gal" may still be found around Salisbury, England.

A priest at heart, Edgar Cayce seldom introduced a person

to a previous incarnation without passing along some solid advice to help in overcoming incurred karma. "These are those experiences that are to be met within self in the present," he gently prodded Mrs. Simmons. "Not what would be termed foolish egotism, but that innate feeling within self that it knows it knows, irrespective of whatever anyone else may say." He urged that she maintain the attitude. "Thy will, O Lord, be done in and through me," and he further admonished:

"In using those experiences, let not thyself grow angry, with thine own self or with others, but manifest meekness, humbleness. Lift up thine eyes to Him Who is the way, and He will ever say as of old, 'Neither do I condemn thee.' For when He forgiveth, it is also forgotten. Look to Him, for He may put into thy activities that which will keep thee daily in the way that speaketh of beauty and charm, that was a part of the experience, and all the waywardness and willfulness will be forgotten."

Mrs. Simmons asked if she had been associated with her present husband in that lifetime, and Cayce replied that he had been an acquaintance who was "always just out of reach of the entity." Intimating that she had been angered by his indifference, Cayce added, "Stand aside oft and watch yourself go by, and you will not be surprised when you are able to control these little angers that arise at times."

According to the Cayce readings, most of us have lived many hundreds of times in physical bodies, but since no one except a near saint can hope to pay off all accumulated karmic debts in one lifetime, the seer gave information only on those particular incarnations which he said were most directly influencing the present one. Mrs. Simmons was therefore told of five, including sojourns in the Holy Land, prehistoric Egypt, and the "lost continent" of Atlantis.

He said that in Palestine her name was Nimmuo, and that her brother was Lucius, Bishop of the Church in Laodicea. Although Mrs. Simmons was unaware of it at the time of the reading, the sleeping seer had previously identified himself as Lucius, a soldier of fortune who had been rejected as an apostle, but was a kinsman of Luke and a close associate of Paul. No records of Lucius have as yet been found, but if the reading is correct, Beverly Simmons would have been Cayce's sister in two previous lives.

The seer told Mrs. Simmons that she was born to wealthy

Palestinian parents, who by cooperating with Roman occupation authorities were able to enjoy special privileges and educational advantages for their children. Through family contacts she had heard of the strange events transpiring in Jerusalem, including the trial and crucifixion, and the reports that Jesus had risen from the dead and been seen at the Sea of Tiberius. It was natural that sixteen-year-old Nimmuo was eager to talk with those Jews who had actually heard the words of this remarkable man, and experienced His healing; so on learning that Lucius was planning a journey to Jerusalem, she persuaded him to take her along on the trip down the Jordan valley.

Cayce recounted that after passing through Perea they came to the house of Lazarus in Bethany, where they met Mary and Martha, and also "the Mother Mary and the rest of the Family that had been gathered by John, in keeping with that command from the cross." They heard the "wondrous story of Jesus from their own lips," and were present on the day of Pentecost "when the entity heard that speech of Peter, saw John, James and the other Apostles as they sat in awe, when the Spirit had descended as in tongues of fire and sat upon that body of the Twelve."

Because of the soul memory of that experience, Cayce said, Beverly Simmons still feels deep reverence for all forms of spiritual phenomena, and often wishes to be alone "to listen to the consciousness within, to hear again that story of those who had known that awareness of His peace." According to the reading, Nimmuo remained for some time there before returning to Laodicea, where she "became an enigma" to her parents, Sophia and Philippe, who could not understand the marked change in their daughter, until Paul and Barnabas later converted them.

Cayce declared that after Lucius was named a bishop, Nimmuo also became a power in church activities; but by siding with her brother in a dispute with Paul, she became involved in conditions which threatened a division of the Early Church and "caused that saint in Patmos to declare, 'I will spew thee out.'" He said Nimmuo eventually brought order and discipline to the Church by treading where others would have feared to tread and admonishing some who were her senior, because, "having received that conviction, that purpose, that ideal from those experiences in Bethany, in the home of the Mother of the Lord . . . the entity stood as a mighty power, alone with the truth in the lack of condemnation to any."

The reading declared that at age twenty-four Nimmuo married "one of the newer converts," a Roman political adviser in Palestine, who has since reincarnated as Riley Simmons, Beverly's present husband. In summarizing the value of the Palestinian experience, Cayce concluded: "Keep in the present ever close to that as ye so oft sought through that experience; to go aside and to put self in the place of those from whom ye heard, and by and through whom ye experienced that ability to bring harmony into the hearts and minds of those disturbed from any cause. And hold fast to that faith as ye expressed oft: so much good in all, none may bear to speak evil of any."

Unusually strong karmic ties seemingly bound Mrs. Simmons to Edgar Cayce, for the readings declared that when he was Uhjltd, a tribal desert leader and mystic in ancient Persia, she was a member of the household; and in prehistoric Egypt, as a priestess named Tar-Ello, she worked closely with the high priest Rata, whom Cayce had once been. The sleeping seer said that for many years before her birth, Rata had been experimenting with ways to improve the human race, which then bore many physical imperfections such as appendages and hooves, and for that purpose he had established a Temple of Sacrifice and a Temple Beautiful to remove blemishes of mind, spirit and body. He said that Tar-Ello's parents had so prepared themselves under the priest's tutelage that she was the first Egyptian child to be born virtually free of blemishes, and with blue eyes and fair skin.

Cayce said that Tar-Ello's mate was Ex-Der-Enemus, the official "insurer" for Egyptian workmen injured or killed in governmental construction work, and that insurance protection for families of workers engaged in hazardous enterprise was then new to the world. Thus, Ex-Der-Enemus wielded great power, working closely with King Aarraat and Ajax, whom Cayce said built the Pyramids. When the seer identified Ex-Der-Enemus as Riley Simmons, Beverly's husband, she was struck by the similarity of interests, since in this life he has pursued a successful career in the mutual insurance field.

Cayce commented that during the latter part of the Tar-Ello incarnation, Beverly "gave way to material things and self-indulgences . . . which brought regrets," and that next to jealousy, nothing saps the spiritual purpose of life like regret. He said that we must firmly put aside any regrets, because when God forgives, the misdeed is also forgotten. He added that because of her high position and near perfection in ancient Egypt, a latent "worshipfulness" is felt toward her by some of those entities living today who had worked with her in the temple, and that they would tend to pattern themselves after her in habits, speech and activities. The moral was obvious. She must so conduct herself in this lifetime as to set a shining example.

XI

Perchance to Dream

MRS. WILFRED SECHRIST of Houston, Texas, was living in Englewood, New Jersey, in 1943 when she first learned of Edgar Cayce through the book *There Is a River*. The idea of reincarnation was novel to her, but because of her bright, inquiring mind she decided to request a life reading. Elsie had been a head nurse at Bellevue Hospital in New York City before her marriage, and after setting up housekeeping in an Englewood apartment she utilized her unaccustomed leisure by showing other young matrons in the building how to mix baby formulas, keep house properly, and prepare nutritious meals. When the transcript of her Cayce reading arrived, stating that she should be an instructor "in the way, the truth and the light," she could not understand what it meant, unless it was referring to her helpfulness to young mothers. As she read on, however, her amazement grew.

Cayce, while in trance, had described four previous lifetimes which he said were most directly related to the purposes for which she entered the present incarnation. After the initial shock, she had to agree that they struck responsive chords within her. In the most recent one prior to her present incarnation, Cayce saw her as an early settler in Provincetown, Massachusetts, where, because of her sympathy with the Indians, she often served as liaison between fellow villagers and the surrounding tribes. Her name, coincidentally, was said to have been Elsie Gilchrist, and when her husband later visited that area, he found that a street in that small town was called Gilchrist, and that the name was a fairly common one there. Elsie readily conceded that since early childhood she has always rooted for the Indians in movies, feeling that they were sadly mistreated and misunderstood by the white men.

The sleeping Cayce further reported that as a child in Palestine "when Christ walked the earth," she had not personally known Jesus, but had worked closely with His followers and witnessed the persecutions of early Christians. The reading stated that she joined the Essenes, even though she was not Jewish, and aided others in interpreting the teachings of Jesus through portions of the Holy Land.

"Perhaps this could explain," Mrs. Sechrist says, "why I became unduly excited on first reading of the discovery of the Qumran ruins on the shores of the Dead Sea. I innately knew Mr. Cayce was right when he said that women as well as men had belonged to the Essene Order there, and although I have no proof, I strongly sense that the left door was the entrance used by females."

At the time of this reading in 1943, no one knew the location of the ruins, and the few historical references to Essene communities indicated that they were exclusively male. Yet as early as 1936, Cayce had told another woman that she had been a sister superior in the Essene Order which was located "on the road above Emmaus, near the road that goes down towards Jericho and towards the northernmost coast from Jerusalem." In 1951 the remains of an Essene community, Qumran, were excavated precisely where Cayce had indicated, and the skeletons of women as well as men were found in surrounding graves. It was at Qumran that the Dead Sea Scrolls, subsequently unearthed in nearby caves, had been written.

Cayce said that Mrs. Sechrist had been a youthful witness on the Day of Pentecost, when the disciples spoke in tongues; yet he had no normal way of knowing about her intense interest in glossolalia during her present lifetime. As a small child, whenever her Sunday school teacher mentioned speaking in tongues Elsie had seemed to see visions of Peter addressing travelers from many lands, each of whom heard the stirring words in his own language; and as an adult she had read considerably on the subject.

The incarnation which reportedly exerts the most powerful influence on her present lifetime was a sojourn as Lido-La in ancient Persia. Cayce said that she was a prophetess and head nurse in "the city in the hills and the plains," and Mrs. Sechrist recalls that upon reading that she had been a sand-reader who migrated from India, "A bell-like sound rang in my head and reverberated up and down my spine." Several years before the Cayce reading, she had attended a motion picture entitled *The Garden of Allah*, in which the hero approached an Indian sand-reader to have his forture told. As Elsie watched the unfolding scene she found herself trembling, "and a light seemed to explode in my brain while I 'identified' with the sand-reader." She says that she has never had this peculiar reaction while watching movies about crystal-ball gazers or gypsies, but she has since developed the faculty of looking into the future for her family. Thus, both the precognitive abilities and the nursing career may be talents developed long ago and reactivated in this lifetime.

The Cayce reading declared that she had been born into India's untouchable caste, but that upon learning from caravan drivers of the greater opportunities for study accorded the underprivileged in Persia, she joined a group that was journeying to "the city in the hills and the plains." Elsie reasons that if one had actually been an untouchable, it would probably help him to appreciate the yearnings of those without opportunity, and says, "I have always championed the unfortunate, but at the time of the reading, I didn't know what Mr. Cayce was talking about. For instance, he said that I had the ability to interpret visions and dreams, because of application along those lines in Persia. I considered that ridiculous! How could I then know that a quarter century later I would have a book published by Cowles Publications on the significance and meaning of dreams?" Entitled *Dreams—Your Magic Mirror*, Elsie Sechrist's recent book is generally regarded as a classic in its field.

Cayce said that during her Persian experience she was placed in charge of all groups of seekers after spiritual knowledge, who came from the Gobi lands, Saad, Greece, Egypt and Persia, instructing them in the spiritual and the mundane. Had Cayce asserted that she would resume this type of work in her present lifetime, she would have laughed

at his folly, but for the past ten years she has served as
director of all study groups for the Association for Research
and Enlightenment (the Edgar Cayce training program), and
has lectured here and abroad on the nature of man as it re-
lates to his psychic capacities, with emphasis on dreams,
prayer and the expansion of consciousness.

Cayce stressed her need to remain humble, cautioning
against any temptation to follow a course that would exalt
her in name or fame, and cited an altercation with her son in
the Persian lifetime which caused her to become angry and
"lose ground" spiritually. "Though ye were abused, though ye
were forgotten," the reading declared, "ye finally returned to
humility of mind that others might know." Although the
meaning of the odd phraseology puzzled Elsie at the time,
she says that it has helped her immeasurably in the years
since, because, "There have been times when, deciding that
others were going about something the wrong way, I resolved
to have nothing more to do with them or their organization.
Then I would remember that this was a lack of humility on
my part, for who is perfect?"

"A dear friend of mine decided to quit the A.R.E. for similar reasons," she continued, "and had actually written her
letter of resignation, when she happened to open her Bible to
this passage in Revelation: 'Be watchful, and strengthen the
things which remain, that are ready to die; for I have not
found thy works perfect before God.' I keep harkening back
to that, realizing that where there are weaknesses, support is
needed, rather than self-righteousness. Certainly it is no time
to run away, for it is God Whom I am trying to serve, and
surely I can't have anything against Him!"

Cayce told Mrs. Sechrist that she had been associated with
him when he was Rata, a high priest in prehistoric Egypt, at
a time when he was establishing higher awareness in consciousness, and that many of the people who worked with
him then had unconsciously found their way back to him and
the work of A.R.E. in this lifetime. Elsie's name then was
said to have been Ist-Hean, and she became a teacher of "the
way, the truth and the light," working with people who came
from all parts of the then-known world to study at the Temple Beautiful near Heliopolis. The entranced seer said that
before entities became eligible to work in that temple, which
emphasized spiritual truths, they had first to graduate from
the Temple of Sacrifice, a type of hospital where inmates

learned about nutrition, control of the lower nature, posture, and exercise, and where surgery was performed. Thus, he indicated that Elsie had learned the fundamentals of nursing in Egypt, as well as in Persia and modern-day New York City.

"The reading warned me about planetary influences from Uranus, which, because of past excesses, could induce me to go to extremes at times," Mrs. Sechrist recalls. "It stressed that I must apply in this lifetime the rules for care of the body that I had learned in ancient Egypt. This could not have been more apropos, because as a young woman I paid no attention to the cries of my body for rest. I felt that I was master of my body, and refused its bid for attention. I was going to finish whatever task I had begun, regardless! Shortly before I heard about Mr. Cayce, I developed a bloodstream infection which settled in the muscles of my heart. The doctor informed my husband that I had no more than five months to live; but a neighbor, Kathryn Baird gave me Richard Ingalese's book, *History and Power of the Mind*. This book changed my attitude toward life and I recovered, but had I not read it, I believe that my own soul would have decided to depart and I would have died."

Cayce taught that the higher self may choose to cut short a life experience, if it feels that the individual self is failing to fufill its purposes for that earthly period, and that we must dissociate God from man-made traits of revenge or punishment. It is not He who decrees that we shall be punished, nor does He decide the time of our death. It is our own activity that builds up the kind of karma that we must meet. If we have taken an eye we must give an eye, unless we have learned never again to repeat such violence. The wanton murder of another, in a previous life, may help to explain why some babies die without apparent physical cause. If a baby is born into a loving family, how better to learn the folly of having taken another's life than to lose this one which he cherishes? Sometimes parental karma may also be involved. The loss of a beloved child may be the result of a parent's suicide in a previous existence, because you cannot just drop love through desertion, and pick it up again. A woman who abandoned her children for a love affair in one life may not be able to give birth in a subsequent one.

A lonely, unattractive woman who yearned for a husband once requested a Cayce reading, and was told that in an earlier life, after her husband had deserted her, she angrily vowed never to fall in love again. She was now said to be paying for her vengeful attitude by being unattractive to the opposite sex. Another reading declared that in a previous incarnation a woman lost her children in a fire, turned against God, and vowed never again to become a mother. In this lifetime she is barren. A married couple with several normal youngsters was appalled to learn that the youngest was a Mongoloid. They asked Cayce why this should happen to them, and the reading asserted that they were "chosen because of your love, compassion and understanding, which enables you to help this soul find its way back" from a previous life of wrongdoing. He cautioned them not to view this experience as punishment, but rather as an opportunity to enrich their own souls through helping this soul imprisoned in a helpless body.

Mrs. Sechrist was so intrigued by her life reading that she went to Virginia Beach to attend a seminar, and as she walked into the Cayce headquarters for the first time, she says that an inner voice told her, "You have come home. You need seek no longer." Almost immediately she saw a woman of whom she says, "I could scarcely take my eyes from hers. I felt that if only I could gaze long enough into her eyes, I would know many things." Groping for courage, she introduced herself to Florence Edmonds, and told her of the odd sensation. Mrs. Edmonds replied that others had mentioned a similar feeling, and that since she was to have a reading that afternoon, she would ask for an explanation. The sleeping Cayce told her that this was a "remembrance of the soul from the Egyptian period," when she had been gatekeeper of the Temple Beautiful, psychically reading soul purposes of those who sought entrance. He said that among them were the present Elsie Sechrist and others, who subconsciously remembered the experience.

Mrs. Sechrist attended the opening class, together with some fifty other seekers, and during his lecture Cayce asked if anyone wanted help with meditation. Although Elsie did not know the meaning of the word, she eagerly raised her hand, and Cayce said that he would awaken her at two A.M. Disappointment edged her voice as she replied that there was no telephone in her room, but the seer said that he would not need one.

"I began to wonder what in the world I had gotten myself into," she laughingly recalls. "Was this perfect stranger going to appear at my bedroom door at such an unseemly hour?"

That night she fell asleep at the usual time, but awakened abruptly and glanced at her luminous wristwatch. It was precisely two A.M. She recalled Cayce's promise, and although she had no conception of how to meditate, she decided to "close my eyes and think about God." Suddenly she says, "I became aware of a field of orange, with one large blue eye looking at me. All I could do was look back at it. What it signified I did not know, but there it was; and then the aroma of gardenias filled the room. Both the fragrance and the eye remained for about fifteen minutes, when I fell asleep. The next morning my roommate asked if by any chance I had smelled gardenias during the night, and I silently blessed her, for I was beginning to question my sanity."

Mrs. Sechrist was eager to tell Cayce about the odd occurrence, but when she rushed up to him before class, he motioned her to silence, saying, "First let me tell you about the dream that I had before awakening you. I dreamed that we were walking in a garden, and you asked me for help in meditation. I said that you must meditate through the all-seeing eye [the pituitary] and you said, 'That's not enough. I also need the odor of gardenias.' "

Elsie says that since then she has always tried to keep fresh gardenias, or incense approximately their fragrance, close to her when she meditates, because it "aids in dissociating my mind from external things and takes me more rapidly into a higher spiritual consciousness."

In the ensuing days, Cayce continued to awaken her through some mysterious process, at the same early morning hour. Then, during her return trip to New Jersey by overnight boat, she awakened and discovered that it was twenty-minutes past two o'clock. She assumed that she had been too tired for Cayce to rouse, but she nevertheless quieted her mind in an attempt to meditate.

"Unexpectedly, I was confronted with a vision of Edgar Cayce's face," she recalls, "and he seemed to be laughing heartily at me. I was so puzzled that as soon as I reached home I telephoned him long-distance to ask what was cooking. He chuckled that he had been amused by my consternation at having overslept, when in truth he himself had been the tardy one in awakening."

During the course of a subsequent life reading, Elsie asked the entranced Cayce whether she and her husband were associated in any previous lives, and he replied, "Many times."

Declaring that the present Wilfred Sechrist was the son with whom she had quarreled in the Persian incarnation, he said, 'In Persia, ye warred one with another. In the present how has it been given? Patience, kindness, gentleness, long-suffering, brotherly love. These manifest the more in thy relationship with thy companion."

"Is it any wonder," Elsie asks, "that after such heated arguments only a few thousand years ago, sparks occasionally still fly between Bill and me today? Mr. Cayce said that I had held positions of authority in many lives, and as a result I was too prone now to rush forward and take charge, rather than inviting others to work with me. I realized that he had correctly analyzed one of my worse failings, and I have since tried to be more patient with others in giving them opportunities to serve."

Edgar Cayce repeatedly stressed the importance of dreams, saying that some of them may be purposeful "soul memories," which rekindle and set in motion constructive ideas and latent abilities. Some years after his demise, Mrs. Sechrist had an unusually vivid dream. Fields of matured wheat waved gently in the breeze, grapes hung heavy on the vine, and the orchards were ripe with fruit. Above it all was the shadow of Jesus, and a voice spoke, saying, "Bring me to the people." It seemed to her like a summons to spread the message of "the way, the truth and the light."

She soon began lecturing and teaching for the A.R.E., and some months later she dreamed that she was speaking in an outdoor amphitheater. Her skin was brown, her feet were shod in sandals, and she wore a brown robe corded at the waist. Torches lighted the arena, and as she sounded a warning that destruction would come unless people changed their selfish ways, a bejeweled woman in the upper tiers began to laugh derisively. Elsie, enraged, said to the woman, "And you will die tomorrow." The woman paled, and Elsie awakened, horrified at her pronouncement of vengeance. She then prayed fervently for forgiveness and understanding.

Two months later, while sharing the lecture platform in San Francisco with Thomas Sugrue, she spoke on spiritual healing. During her address a beautifully gowned woman persisted in tittering and laughing sarcastically. Anger welled up inside of Mrs. Sechrist, but suddenly she remembered the dream and, breathing a prayer, stopped in mid-sentence to declare, "There is something that we all need constantly to remember; that people are like flowers in the garden of God. Many are like buds, with their hearts tightly closed to the sun, not yet giving of their beauty and fragrance. Others already like full-blown roses, with souls open to the sun, receiving the light and giving it to all who pass by. But the important thing to remember is that all people are as children in the garden of God." Then she resumed her lecture. When she had finished, the woman who had thought spiritual healing so excruciatingly funny came forward, abjectly apologized for her ill-bred interruptions, and said that the idea of people being like flowers in God's garden had opened for her a whole new world of thought. She became a regular attendant during the remainder of the seminar. Elsie says that she does not know the source of her impromptu statement, but believes it to have been an answer to her unspoken prayer, which perhaps erased for her a karmic debt. Whether the dream of the amphitheater was an actual recall from a past life, or a precognitive warning of an impending challenge cannot be known, but she feels that it prepared her to meet a weakness within herself.

As Elsie continued her daily meditation, she sensed an expansion of consciousness during waking and dreaming hours, which enabled her better to understand herself and others. One day, while attending a preview of the motion picture *King Solomon's Mines* in Hollywood, a scene showing Watusi dancers flashed on the screen, and she had an almost uncontrollable desire to leap into the aisle. "I felt that I could easily do that dance," she explains, "the graceful leap, the circling head and stomping feet. Accompanying the inner exuberance was a feeling of elation and happiness, so that I was thrilled to the core of my being. That night in a dream, I found myself a Watusi; a woman, tall, dark and graceful leading a group of chanting women out of a round, thatched-straw temple. The chant was in a foreign tongue, but as I awakened with its vibrations still in my throat, I heard myself say, 'These are my beloved people.' "

Reviewing the experience, she says, "I have always felt deep kinship with Africans, especially the Watusis. Long before seeing the movie I had avidly read everything that I could about them, and had considered them the noblest people on earth. Believing that I may once have been a Watusi helps me to understand the warmth of my feelings for African women. Edgar Cayce's readings said that all of us have had life experience in many races, countries and religions, and one reading declared that George Washington Carver was previously a highly developed Caucasian who chose to return as an American Negro, to help that race through difficult times."

Elsie recognizes that she must constantly be on guard against a sense of impatience with those who do not measure up to her own standards. This was particularly true with a member of her family, and before falling asleep one night she kept repeating to herself, "Why won't she learn? Why won't she learn?" The Cayce readings suggest that dreams in which the participants are clad in costumes of another era are apt to be soul memories, and that night Elsie's dream took her to an Early American period in which today's relative was a friend. "I realized," she says, "that the activities and status in the life I was witnessing were such that she had made tremendous forward strides in her present lifetime. I felt that the purpose of this glimpse into her past was not only to show me that she had correspondingly progressed more rapidly than I, but to remind me that we must not judge others."

Several years ago, Elsie dreamed that she was inspecting cavelike homes in a hillside community, and demonstrating the art of cleanliness to a primitive people with low foreheads, flat heads and long, straight black hair. In the next scene she found herself with Edgar Cayce in another cavelike dwelling, where he was cleansing the wound of a native and she was assisting him. On awakening, she realized that she had recognized Cayce as the doctor, even though he resembled the other natives. Unable to fathom the dream, she mentioned it to Hugh Lynn Cayce, who said that she had apparently described the Persian "city in the hills and the plains," where many people dwelt in such caves. As Lido-La she was said to have worked closely with Edgar Cayce, who was a shaman called Uhjltd, and the readings further said that present-day Shushtar, Iran, occupies the site of what was then the "city in the hills and the plains." Perhaps, then, it was in that lifetime that Elsie laid the groundwork for her love of cleanliness, neatness and orderliness in the home, which she tried to instill in those young matrons in Plainfield, New Jersey.

Coincidentally, an Iranian exchange student at a college in Houston was recently invited to share Thanksgiving dinner with the Sechrists, and as he walked into their living room, he started in surprise at one of Elsie's amateur paintings framed on the wall. He eagerly asked from what she had copied it, and on being told that the scene was purely imaginary, having been drawn from her own subconscious, he exclaimed, "But that is an exact picture of our summer resort town, Shushtar, in Iran!"

Three successive dreams seemed to Elsie to place her in what is called the lost continent of Atlantis. Time, Edgar Cayce insisted, is not a line drawn out to infinity, but a dimension of consciousness; and since all thoughts, deeds and events have been recorded on the skein of time and space, a person through meditation can develop the art of tuning in on these akashic records, much as we can replay old tape recordings. If true, it would be possible to tap into memories from prehistoric lifetimes as well as more recent ones.

In these dream sequences, Elsie says that she was "aware" of being in Atlantis. In the first scene she was watching a woman floating around in the sky, in what appeared to be a wicker basket, from which observational vantage point she was patrolling the fairgrounds below. The men looked somewhat like our Eskimos, with reddish skin and shiny black hair, and in the distance she could see large granite buildings of a city. When Elsie first told me of the dream, I considered it so lacking in significance that I did not intend to include it in this book. Several months later, however, the North American Newspaper Alliance carried a syndicated article about "The Year 2000; A Framework for Speculation on the Next 33 Years," by Herman Kahn and Anthony J. Wiener, which stated: "The extraordinary look ahead is based on a long-term study at one of the nation's brainiest think-tanks, the Hudson Institute, Inc. at Croton-on-Hudson, N.Y." The report identified Kahn as a physicist and mathematician, and Wiener as chairman of the Research Management Council at the Hudson Institute; and among the innovations which these two scholars considered "very likely" before the end of this century were "individual flying platforms." After reading the article, I recalled that three decades ago Edgar Cayce had declared that Atlanteans were beginning to be reborn in great numbers, to achieve technological advancements which were well known to them before Atlantis disappeared into the sea. Had Elsie Sechrist, after all, relived a dream memory of a woman alone in a basketlike affair, without propellers, policing the area below?

In her second "Atlantean" dream, Elsie had just learned of

the death of her husband and ten children in a fire, and was overcome with grief. A man whom she recognized as her present husband was trying to comfort her, as they walked together up a hillside adjoining a large excavation. She says of the experience, "My grief was so intense that even after I awakened, Bill had difficulty in bringing me back to the reality of today."

The third dream occurred following a lecture. A man from the audience had come up to congratulate her, and she unexpectedly found herself recoiling, as if fearful that he might touch her. That night during sleep she found herself in a large granite house in Atlantis, alone in her bed, when the man whom she had met at the lecture broke down the door and assaulted her. Elsie is convinced that this event actually occurred in ages past, and that it explains why, although she is by nature courageous, she always pushes a chair against her locked bedroom door before retiring, if her husband is not with her. Whether this is imagination or memory, we have no present way of knowing.

A woman whom the Sechrists had met only briefly once invited them to be weekend guests at her estate in Ojai, California. As her hostess came downstairs the first evening, Elsie exclaimed over an unusually large, dark purple amethyst ring on her finger. On learning that Elsie's birthdate was February 12, the woman said, "Then this is your birthstone, and for some reason I feel that I should give you the ring." And she did.

That night Elsie dreamed that she was seated on the balustrade of a gray stone house in England, beside a close friend who was pouring out her woes. The friend's daughter had married against her parents' wishes, and the son-in-law had been arrested for stealing. As the dreamer sought to comfort the other woman, she recognized her as the hostess whom she barely knew, and heard these words: "The ring is a debt of gratitude from that lifetime."

She was so puzzled that the next morning, without mentioning the dream, she asked her hostess what foreign country she would choose for residence if she were not an American. Without hesitation, the much-traveled woman replied, "Oh, England. That is my second home!" Elsie feels that her hostess must also have had a subconscious memory of that lifetime in England, when they had been close friends, for Cayce said that our emotional reactions to people and places often indicate meaningful memories of past life experiences.

Perhaps Elsie's most intriguing dream was one in which she saw the symbol of a heart, within which was engraved "Saskia," and as she returned to consciousness, she heard the words, "You were Saskia." The name meant nothing to her, and had the dream been less vivid she would probably have put it from her mind. Some weeks later, however, she chanced to ask an artist friend, Berenice Wyatt, if she had ever heard a name like Saskia, and the friend responded, "Yes, that was Rembrandt's wife. I particularly remember, because I have a book containing the published papers of the physician who took care of her until she died." Berenice rushed home to find the book, *Rembrandt,* by Van Loon, and telephoned to say excitedly, "There's a picture in the front of the book, of Saskia sitting on Rembrandt's lap, and it's you, Elsie. It looks just like you!"

Mrs. Sechrist, after borrowing the book to read, said of it, "I was astonished to note how many qualities, both good and bad, I share with a woman who lived three hundred years ago. Saskia loved food, and was consequently overweight. This is a problem that I have to work at all the time. Rembrandt was a spendthrift, and Saskia had inherited a large fortune. Therefore, when she realized that death was near, she willed the estate to Rembrandt on condition that he not remarry. She may have hoped that in this way there would be enough money left to educate their infant son, or was it jealousy?" Elsie ruefully admits that she, too, has a tendency to give with strings attached, unless she sternly disciplines herself.

Saskia's doctor reported that although she was patient in most things, tiny noises like the rustling of paper or tapping of fingers nearly drove her to distraction. "You need only ask my husband whether this is not also true of me," Elsie says. Saskia had beautiful hands, and Elsie's hands have often been admired. Saskia was a student of the Bible, as is Elsie, and both believed in reincarnation.

"Like Saskia," Elsie says, "I have no real gift for painting, but love art so much that I haunt the galleries, and my favorites are Rembrandt and Da Vinci. Saskia had many portraits painted by Rembrandt, for he often used her as a model, and she sat patiently by the hour, scarcely moving a muscle. Long before my eerie dream, Mignon Du Broff, a New York artist who painted my portrait, commented that I was the only nonprofessional model with whom she had ever worked who could sit hour after hour without squirming.

"Saskia died of tuberculosis at the age of twenty-four. As a nurse in New York I specialized in tuberculosis cases, and was in charge of a TB ward until a dream warned me to avoid active cases, because of an inherent susceptibility to TB in myself. A brother and sister of mine both had tuberculosis.

"A strange incident occurred in 1966 when my husband and I went to Amsterdam, and visited the home in which Rembrandt and Saskia had lived. We walked through several rooms until we reached one in the back, which displays many of his prints. Without warning, I was overcome by a feeling of depression and suffocation, and as I was wondering whether I should leave, the guide remarked, 'This is the room where Rembrandt's wife died. It was then the bedroom.'"

XII

Spontaneous Recall

EACH of us was born into a particular family, race, and nationality, with seemingly no choice in the matter. Some have healthy bodies, brilliant minds, and loving parents whose wealth makes it possible for then to pursue education and the arts. Others may be born into squalor, indifference, or depravity, further handicapped by blindness, or a low I.Q. Why should there be such a capricious distribution of opportunity and talent, if God is truly just and all-loving?

Some clergymen try to keep their flocks content by preaching that everything will be evened-up on the other side, but it is questionable whether the more thoughtful ones really believe what they are saying. If each of us has but a single earth span, why should dullards and geniuses, Mongoloid idiots and infant prodigies be born haphazardly in various parts of the globe? Is God more cruel than we ourselves would be in dispensing welfare?

Only if each soul has lived numerous times before can such gross inequities be explained in light of the previous uses made of equal opportunities. This is cause and effect—the law of karma—and God remains a wise and loving Creator if we accept the philosophy that it is not He who punishes us with inferior minds or bodies, but we ourselves who chose them in order to seek atonement for past misdoings. Plato, who taught the doctrine of reincarnation, advanced the theory that those things which we learn easily were known to us before, whereas knowledge which is difficult to assimilate is being encountered by us for the first time in this lifetime. Who can forget radio's famous "Quiz Kids," who mentally solved mathematical equations that many adults could not calculate even with paper and pencil? Why is it that Beethoven and Mozart could compose brilliant symphonies in their childhood, when so few of us play really well even after many years of music lessons? Some of our musical geniuses were born into musical families, so that heredity could be a factor, but many others were not. Did they, then, bring a knowledge of music with them into this life?

The fact that most of us fail to remember past lives need not seem so strange, when we consider how many times our memory has failed us in this life. I "know" that I was born in Sumner, Illinois, although my birth was not officially recorded, and I recall nothing of having lived there. I accept it as fact because my parents and grandparents said that it was so. My first recollections date from the age of three, after we had moved from Sumner, but I by no means remember everything that happened to me at that age. Why cannot I remember more than a few isolated incidents, if I was as alive at three as I am now? The argument that my mind was not then fully developed cannot provide the whole explanation, because I have since forgotten the names of countless fellow students and teachers in high school and college, together with considerable book learning and innumerable incidents.

As I grow older, I forget numerous happenings of much more recent vintage, and fail to recall some of them even when reminded by others of my participation. None of us can retain everything in our minds, which automatically weed out much trivia, and also some knowledge that we would like to have kept, but it is never actually lost. This has been scientifically proven under hypnosis. Our subconscious has simply filed it away, and a hypnotist can tap into that storehouse by regressing us to a particular age and place, and asking us to relate what is transpiring. It therefore becomes obvious that although specific details are often forgotten, we retain the experience gained by those incidents, and profit accordingly. A toddler who burned his hand on a heater cannot remember the actual pain, but he will thereafter avoid coming into physical contact with one that is lighted. In the same way, it seems logical that we can carry forward with us the wisdom and experience acquired in previous lifetimes, even though we do not recall the incidents which gave us that knowledge. To do so, in our present state of development, would unnecessarily clutter our minds and leave little room for acquiring new knowledge.

Some people bitterly resent the idea of a law of karma, arguing that one lifetime is quite enough, and that they prefer to look forward to an eternity in a beautiful heaven. But what if we assumed the same attitude toward the law of gravitation? We may dislike the idea that if we step off a high building we will fall to the ground, but disbelieving this basic law of the universe does not change it. Since we are fully conscious of many of our sins of omission and commission, it should be reassuring to think that we will be given another chance before "Judgment Day." The widespread fear of dying may be attributable to the fact that many people, visualizing the Sunday school lessons of childhood, dread to approach some remote "judgment seat" where they will be eternally consigned to the spot that they have earned for themselves, in Heaven or Hell.

How much more comforting to believe that our souls are their own judge of good and evil, that God loves us all equally, and that through His mercy we will be granted as many lifetimes as we choose in which to atone for our waywardness. We may deceive others, but we cannot deceive ourselves. We are our own judge and jury, so it is time that we stopped whimpering about the cruel fate that cast us in an unwanted role. The doctrine of reincarnation teaches that in most instances we ourselves selected that role, and if we would prefer to have a pleasanter one in the next go-round, now is the time to begin earning it by understudying the saints. Every thought and word and deed of ours is being firmly implanted on the record of our souls. Each time that we forgive another and lend him a helping hand, we are canceling out some of the debit in our ledger.

By no means all of the poor and afflicted have incurred worse karma in previous lives than those who are now affluent and healthy. If it is true that we ourselves ordinarily select the circumstances into which we are born, some may deliberately have chosen the lot of the underprivileged in order to learn needed lessons, and to pay off an accumulation of debts more rapidly than those who are trying to work off only a few past mistakes in the present lifetime. This is the error which has crept into some Oriental faiths. On seeing an "untouchable" desperately struggling to save himself from drowning, a Hindu may turn the other way, saying, "It is his karma. In a previous life he doubtless took another's life." That Hindu overlooks the possibility that it may have been his own karma to pass along the shore as another is drowning, and by risking his own life, to save him, thereby acquiring God's grace. It is not our privilege to judge another.

"Love thy neighbor as thyself" was not spoken idly. It was a command, which we ignore at our own risk. The backward boy or struggling laborer in this incarnation may be our leader, our employer, or our parent in the next. Certainly, according to the philosophy of reincarnation, we will be irrevocably tied to anyone whom we have wronged until our indebtedness is repaid.

Edgar Cayce, while in sleeplike state, gave two sources for his out-of-the-world knowledge: the subject's subconscious, which remembers all of its acts; and the collective unconscious, or akashic records on which are indelibly written all thoughts and deeds since the beginning of mankind. For forty-two years, until his death in 1945, Cayce was seemingly able to tap both of these reservoirs. All that he needed to know was the name and approximate location of the person for whom he read. Most of his subjects were strangers at a distance, and although it is impossible to prove his readings about their previous incarnations, so much of his other material did check out that thousands of clergymen, doctors, professors and laymen who studied his work changed from skeptics to believers.

Hugh Lynn Cayce, who directs the monumental task of indexing and substantiating his father's many thousands of readings, says without qualification, "I believe that Dad's life readings were even more accurate than his physical readings." This is a remarkable statement, inasmuch as the accuracy of most of his physical readings has astounded physicians and laymen for three generations.

A businessman once challenged Cayce to trace his steps to his office in New York City, while the seer lay in trance at Virginia Beach. On receiving the report later in the week, the man was nonplussed. Cayce not only had "seen" him stop to purchase two cigars at a tobacco store, and walk rather than take the elevator to his office, but he had even read his morning mail.

The scientific community paid scant attention to Cayce's psychic powers before his death, except to note his diagnostic and healing powers; but psychologists and psychiatrists are beginning to take a new look at his life readings, because of the work which Dr. Ian Stevenson, recently retired chairman of the Department of Neurology and Psychiatry at the University of Virginia, has been doing in the field of reincarnation. In his documented book, *Twenty Cases Suggestive of Reincarnation,* Dr. Stevenson recounts his personal investigation of children who at an early age began talking of a previous life lived in a locality with which they could not be personally familiar. Many of the youngsters have given such a wealth of detail about obscure happenings, and supplied so many names of people whom they claimed as former relatives, that they have attracted scientific interest.

On March 16, 1964, Dr. Stevenson first met Imad Elawar, a five-year-old boy living in the village of Kornayel, near Beirut, Lebanon. The youngster had for several years been asserting that he was formerly a member of a Bouhamzy family in Khriby, another Lebanese village separated from Kornayel by a mountain. The boy frequently mentioned "Jamile," a "beautiful" woman for whom he expressed great fondness; and he also gave the names of a sister, a brother, and other relatives and friends of the Bouhamzy he claimed to have been.

During that trip to Lebanon, Dr. Stevenson learned that a Khriby man named Ibrahim Bouhamzy had died of tuberculosis at the age of twenty-five, nine years before Imad's birth. Although the latter had never been to Khriby, or met anyone from that village, Ibrahim seemed to fit the boy's description of his former self, even to having had a mistress named Jamile. Dr. Stevenson was fortunate in being able to accompany Imad and his father on their first trip to Khriby, during which the lad pointed across a valley toward the house where he claimed to have lived, and also to the village where Jamile had resided at that time. He failed to recognize houses in the immediate vicinity of his old neighborhood, but neighbors verified that their appearance had been considerably altered during the intervening years.

Imad further failed to recognize Ibrahim's mother, who by then was an old woman, but he correctly identified Ibrahim's sister Huda by name, recognized a large oil painting as a portrait of his brother Fuad, and a photograph of Ibrahim Bouhamzy as "me," despite the fact that those present had tried to mislead him by suggesting that it was an uncle. Asked by Huda to repeat the last words spoken on "his" deathbed, Imad correctly responded, "Huda, call Fuad." He also indicated where his dog and gun had been kept, and where his bed formerly stood; and claimed to have owned a small yellow automobile, a bus, a rifle, a double-barreled shotgun, and other personal items. These statements were verified by members of the Bouhamzy family and their friends. Imad's parents and grandparents had previously remarked on the unusual surprise and joy that the child evinced on learning to walk, almost as if he could not believe the phenomenon, and Dr. Stevenson learned that Ibrahim had been bedridden during the last months of his life. Dr. Stevenson was also able to determine that Imad's parents had tried to discourage him from his claims of a previous life, which he began asserting at the age of eighteen months. He could find no evidence of fraud, since both the Elawar and Bouhamzy families are highly respected for integrity in their respective communities, and each had been unknown to the other.

A case which attracted considerable newspaper interest in 1937 was that of Shanti Devi, a Hindu girl who at the age of four began referring to incidents of a previous life in which, she insisted, she had been a Choban by caste. She claimed that her husband was Pt. Kedar Nath Chaubey, a cloth merchant living some distance away in Muttra, and she supplied much detail about her previous home, its décor and arrangement of rooms. She even gave the address, and when her parents finally sent a letter to that name and address, they received a reply from the man whom the child had named. Although he had remarried since his wife's death, he came to Delhi, and Shanti immediately recognized the stranger as her "husband." He then asked her intimate questions about himself and his former household, all of which she reportedly answered correctly. She described the town, and also a temple to which she said she had promised one hundred rupees, the money being buried under the floor of her house.

Fifteen investigators accompanied Shanti to Muttra shortly thereafter, and when the party detrained, she directed the driver how to reach her former home. At the end of a narrow lane, she correctly identified a man as her "father-in-law," and pointed to "her" house. Before entering it, she again described the room arrangement, which turned out to be precisely as she "remembered." She next led the group to a different house in which she claimed to have died, and pointed to the corner of a room where she said she had hidden the money for the church. A hole was dug, and a place for keeping valuables was found, but it was empty. This was the house where Kedar Nath now lived, and he later admitted having removed the money after his wife's death. Shanti also led the way to the home of her former parents and unhesitatingly embraced them, although some fifty other persons were present, and some had tried to trick her by holding out their arms.

Spontaneous recall of previous lifetimes seem to occur much more often in children than adults, perhaps because imposed disciplines and the problems of everyday living have not yet crowded out those illusive memories. Julia Chandler successfully pursued a half-dozen careers, before her death in 1966. She served as drama critic for seven years on the old Washington *Herald,* and had also been a feature writer for the Chicago *Tribune* before David Belasco brought her to New York to direct publicity for the Belasco Theater. A play that she wrote was produced on Broadway. Then, as general manager of the Empire State Observatory, she became known as "the lady in the sky"; and from her perch high above the roar of traffic, in the Empire State tower, she conducted a daily radio program called *Microphone in the Sky.*

Despite the glamour of her multiple careers, Julia Chandler was never able to thrust from her memory a vision which she had glimpsed as a child in Bowling Green, Virginia. Discussing it many years later, she said, "I loved to lie in the cool grass, with half-closed eyes, watching the lights and shadows cast by fluttering leaves of the maple tree overhead. After a long period of this concentrated observation, the tents of my consciousness folded back and I found myself in a Grecian garden."

Trellises with green vines occupied a section of the garden, and at one end of it was a beautiful temple with Ionic columns, she said, and continued, "As I watched entranced, a young girl of about sixteen came out of the temple. She was clothed in a soft, clinging, white Grecian robe which was bound above her waist with a golden cord. Her hair was piled high on her head in soft ringlets banded with gold, and on her feet were golden sandals. She stood for a moment listening to the soft music made by the wind in the tall trees which surrounded the garden. Then she began to dance, and everything in that faraway world seemed to dance with her—the leaves, the sun, my heart—for somehow I knew I was that Grecian maid, although at the time I had no knowledge of reincarnation, nor of the existence of akashic records."

Julia Chandler said that the vision recurred intermittently until she was about eighteen. Then, after a lapse of fifteen years, she saw it again with startling clarity. A few days later she invited Flower Newhouse, a California mystic and lecturer, to appear on her radio broadcast which regularly featured royalty and other celebrities visiting in New York City. The program went smoothly, but afterward Mrs. Newhouse suddenly stared at Julia and said, "You were a temple dancer in Greece five hundred years before the birth of Christ."

Mrs. Chandler managed to conceal her surprise, and in commenting later on the experience, said, "As I had never told anyone at all of my Grecian garden scenes, I realized that it was impossible for Mrs. Newhouse to know about it from any human source. Nor did I tell her at once. I first asked how she knew, whereupon she described the scene which had first been revealed to me under my Virginia maples when I was a little girl, giving a full account of the sixteen-year-old maid who came out of the temple to dance in the sunlit garden. She told me, further, that it was at the time of Pythagoras, and that I had been one of his students during a portion of that incarnation." Subsequently Mrs. Chandler had a reading with Edgar Cayce, who also tuned into that same period, giving her a detailed account of her Grecian lifetime and of its influence on the present one.

It is interesting to note that the past life which Julia Chandler seemed to recall occurred thousands of years ago, whereas those of Shanti Devi and Imad Elawar were of such recent date that their former "mothers" still survived. Edgar Cayce said that three types of entities tend to reincarnate quickly: those who lived good lives until almost the last, when they abruptly erred, and were anxious to correct their errors quickly; those whose lives were cut short, with youthful desires still unfulfilled; and those who had attained high spiritual development, but were willing to come back and help others, rather than accept their earned reward.

He indicated that among those in the second category are

youths who lost their lives in battle, are deeply resentful of the adult bungling that led to war, and rush back without proper preparation to satisfy their physical longings. Some psychics insist that many of today's rioters, draft-card burners, and hippies are reincarnations of soldiers and civilians whose lives were snuffed out through no fault of their own in World War II or the Korean War, and that this explains their defiant attitude toward all authority today.

Living in Norfolk, Virginia, is a young man who since babyhood has been in revolt against all parental discipline. He had barely learned to talk before he was shouting "Heil Hitler," and with his baby blocks he was constantly building tanks which he pushed around the room in a belligerent manner. After starting to school, he spent most of his allowance on paperback books about Hitler, Goering, Himmler and other Nazis, and he would argue endlessly about the superiority of the Aryan race. "Hitler was right," he would scream at his shocked parents, who tried to explain the folly of his reasoning. Once, observing that his mother was reading Exodus, the boy gave her such a graphic account of the ovens at Dachau that she felt sick at heart.

As a teen-ager the lad became so unmanageable that his parents sent him to a military academy, where he took to army discipline like a duck to water. Without volunteering any information, his mother requested a life reading for him, and the psychic said that in the son's previous incarnation he had been a German soldier who lost his life in World War II. The boy's militaristic bent continued until the age of seventeen. Then, perhaps because he was approaching draft age, he evinced terror whenever Vietnam was mentioned, and announced that he wanted no part of war. "Hitler was a fool," he abruptly told his mother. "Everything that he did was wrong. He started a war." At this writing he is in a reserve unit, and has not yet been called to active duty.

XIII

In Our Reveries

THROUGH dreams, meditation, hypnotic regression, and instantaneous recall, forgotten corridors of the past have seemingly been explored; and there is still another method which has been used with some success. This is a form of reverie in which the subject is led to probe subconscious memories. During the decade of the 1930's, a study group met with the late A. R. Martin in Sharon, Pennsylvania, to make scientific experiments in the field of reincarnation. In the most frequently used procedure, one of the members seated himself directly opposite Martin, and two others placed their fingers on the pulsebeat of the subject's wrist while Martin spoke softly to him, suggesting that the pulse would slow as he gradually relaxed and freed his mind of everyday pressures, until he was opening his subconscious to far-off memories.

During one such session, an American began speaking in fluent German, although in his conscious state he was unfamiliar with that language. A couple present were fortunately able to identify the dialect as one peculiar to an area near Berlin, which they had not heard spoken since coming to America eleven years previously. The subject, in this semiconscious state, said that he was experiencing a life as a soldier in the German army during the seventeenth century, and he graphically described the customs and activities of that period. Then he seemingly relived a still earlier life in which, as a carpenter working on a scaffold which collapsed, he suffered severe injuries which impaired his speech and totally disabled his body. By sputtering and stammering, he managed to express his indignation at a court ruling which denied him compensation, and thereby the means to support himself.

In a privately printed volume, *Researches in Reincarnation and Beyond,* Martin told of one woman in the class who recalled that as a baby, in early pioneering days, she had been stolen by the son of an Indian chief and reared as a member of the tribe. Not until a British trader took her away did she learn that she was white. The trader eventually deserted her, and fearing to live alone or to bear the shame of rejoining the tribe, she shot off the right side of her face with a gun.

The woman, during the reverie state, said that she reincarnated in the body of a cripple whose right side was completely paralyzed; and she sensed that this was a penance necessitated by her previous suicide, to learn appreciation and respect for a healthy body. The next lifetime described was that of an American soldier who, during the Revolutionary War, died from a stab wound in the abdomen. In her reverie, she later saw herself as a girl named Nancy, whose mother was a servant; and when the scion of a wealthy family fell in love with the servant's daughter, his parents objected so strenuously that she was hastily married off to a farmhand, who took his bride to Illinois in a covered wagon. After bearing two children, Nancy died of abdominal disorders, at the age of thirty. Next, she was the beautiful daughter of well-to-do parents living near Baltimore. She said that she became an opera singer, married a prominent lawyer, and moved with him to Philadelphia; but on one of his business trips the lawyer was fatally shot, and she died soon after of a broken heart.

Martin reported that the woman subsequently meditated on each of these lifetimes, coming to understand her inner fears, and then used them to meditate on such needed qualities as courage, love, and tolerance. In her present life she has suffered from abdominal disorders, which she now believes stem from her subconscious remembrance of her deaths as a revolutionary soldier, and as Nancy. She sees that many of her present reactions have been negative, indicating that she has not yet learned lessons taught by previous experience, and this has enabled her to replace tensions with mental pictures of harmony and perfection.

Through the group study, a lad of eleven whose inferiority complex greatly inhibited his performance as a musician was able to review a lifetime in which he had been a noted composer. He gave a wealth of information, including names and dates, which subsequently checked out correctly in reference books. This "awareness" of previous success gave him such inner confidence that he was able to give a brilliant performance with a famous symphony orchestra, when barely into his teens. Thus, it would seem that we can profit by exploring previous lives, if we are willing to use that knowledge in the context of our present behavioral patterns.

Is it possible that Margot Mason of Washington, D.C., is the reincarnation of world-famous astrologer Evangeline Adams of Boston? Pretty, blond Margot does not know, but the parallels are so intriguing that the coincidences deserve consideration. The story begins with her father, Frank McDonough, a New Jersey businessman, who in the late 1950's was leaving on a hurried business trip to Nebraska, and wanted something to read en route. Grabbing up the first book that he saw on a library counter, he boarded the train, and settled back in his seat to read *The Bowl of Heaven* by Evangeline Adams. He had never heard of the author or the title, and to his disgust he discovered that his only reading matter was an autobiography of an astrologer.

McDonough had no interest in the subject, either before or after reading the book, but for some inexplicable reason he felt a compulsion to acquire an extensive library on astrology which Miss Adams stated that she had collected from all parts of the world. On his return East, he learned that Miss Adams had been dead for more than a quarter century; and although no one seemed to know what had become of her library, he set out in determined search of it, haunting secondhand bookstalls in Boston and New York, where she had practiced. His quest continued for three years, before he wandered into a little basement bookstore in Boston. It had only a few books on astrology, but he was so insistent that there were more that the proprietor finally took him to another store, where he had others. McDonough pulled a book from the shelf, and there on the flyleaf was the signature of Evangeline S. Adams. He excitedly pulled down another book, and another, and another. All of them bore her signature.

McDonough acquired her library of nearly four hundred books, and then wondered what in the world to do with it. Like a ravenous man who gorges himself on food, McDonough's strange hunger for the books was now satiated. He had no intention of reading them, some of which were more than four hundred years old and handwritten, and he could ill afford the expenditure that he had made. Ruefully deciding that there was only one solution to his rash extravagance, he was preparing to sell the books when Margot came home for a visit. And now it is her story.

"The moment I saw that library," she exclaims, "I knew that it was for me. It was mine from the instant I entered the room. Like my father, I knew nothing of astrology, and I had rarely read books since my student days at the University of New Mexico, but there was an entire library that I could scarcely wait to devour."

The books so fascinated her that she decided to stay until she had read them all. She took a demanding job as secretary to a criminal lawyer, and would then stay up nearly all night studying astrology from Evangeline's books. Soon she began working up zodiacal charts, and discovered something rather uncanny. She herself not only had the horoscope of an astrologer, but her chart and that of Evangeline Adams combined like a jigsaw puzzle.

"Her sun is on my Seventh House of partnerships," Margot explains. "Her moon is in conjunction with my sun and ascendant. This always causes an unbreakable bond between two people. Attachments between Venus and Saturn in two horoscopes cause an everlasting friendship. Miss Adams' Venus is exactly 'on' my Saturn, the same degree and sign, in my Eighth House—of death! In other words, this bond came after death."

Throughout her library Evangeline Adams left blue-penciled notes, so that as Margot worked with it she could see the famed astrologer's sources, and what she intended to do with the material. She became so engrossed in carrying on Evangeline's work that after saving every cent possible, she took a year's leave of absence from her job, locked herself in her room most of the time, and studied astrology eighteen hours a day. She rarely went out or accepted dates, although she was barely into her twenties. When she ran out of money she would go back on the double schedule, until she could finance herself again for a time.

The McDonoughs moved to Sarasota, Florida, and Margot set up the library there. Having become convinced of the value of astrology in raising children, through character analysis, she began work on a series of books under the general title *What Makes You Tick,* which were published by Gold Star Books. She has also broadcast astrology programs on radio and television stations in Washington, D.C., where she now conducts clssses in astrology.

Unlike Evangeline Adams, whose proper Bostonian family was scandalized by her pursuit of astrology in the Victorian era, Margot comes from a broad-minded family of widely varied hobbies, who respect each other's pursuits. If she is indeed the incarnation of Evangeline, that could explain her choice of parents in this lifetime. Evangeline Adams was born in 1868, and her famous clients included Mary Garden, naturalist John Burroughs, Tallulah Bankhead, Enrico Caruso, and J. P. Morgan. She died in 1932, four years before the birth of Margot McDonough on August 10, 1936, at 5:21 A.M. in Denver, Colorado.

The dovetailing of their horoscopes is doubly interesting in that Margot seems stubbornly to have chosen the moment of her birth. Her mother had an exceedingly difficult pregnancy, and went four times to the hospital on false alarms before the baby finally was delivered. Mrs. McDonough says of this, "When Margot was born, the doctor said in the delivery room that she was a month late, and that my uremic poisoning should have forced an earlier birth. He had expected the baby to be born dead, but I have since wondered whether she delayed her birth until the exact time when she could have the horoscope which would coincide with that of Evangeline Adams."

The young woman who took "Margot Mason" as a professional name says she is convinced that she had divine guidance in learning astrology, adding: "I am totally self-taught, but I have a strange contact with that library. I can feel, by holding out my hand, where the information that I seek will be found. The library now contains nearly a thousand volumes, but if I am looking for something in particular, I simply walk around the room with outstretched hand, until I 'feel' which book to take from the shelf. Then I open it to the precise page containing the information. As I studied those books, it was as if I were taking a refresher course, because I automatically knew the answers. No other kind of learning had ever come this easily to me."

Within three years after she walked into her parents' home and saw the library, seasoned astrologers who questioned her said that few others could have absorbed so much of the knowledge even in thirty years of study. This may indicate that Margot was simply picking up the study where she had left off in a previous time.

XIV

Recalling One's Birth

A MAJORITY of the lives described during hypnotic regression are either too remote in history or too far removed from newsmaking headlines to be verifiable, but when certain assertions prove to be true, we find it easier to accept the remainder of the material as valid. Such is the case of Bertha Jennings Hahn of Newark, Delaware, who served as a hypnotic subject while visiting me in February 1968. After being regressed to the ages of five and two in her present life, she was instructed to go farther back in time, until she found herself in a different body. At the count of twenty-five, she said that she was dancing outside, her hair was dark, and she was dressed from head to toe in white.

"I'm the prima ballerina," she said breathlessly. "I'm taking my third bow . . . my third curtain call. There's to be a dinner in my honor later. It's for the entire cast." She said that the host would be Jacques Bergnac, "the producer of the ballet" that was then performing at an open-air theater in Paris. Giving her name as Colette Dupré, she said that she was twenty years old and the year was 1870.

Moved ahead five years, she said that she was now married to Count Radnor, a wealthy man whom she had met through her producer. "He was a great fan of mine," she declared. Asked if he had been a stage door Johnny, she replied

quickly, "He's much too important for that!" She said that
they had a large house on the Riviera, with servants, and
were deeply in love. Five years later, she still described her
marriage as blissfully happy, and said that they had a two-
year-old son, Jacques; but when taken forward to the age of
fifty, she sobbingly told us, "I'm sad. Alone. My husband
. . . he was drowned." She added that despite her wealth she
had recently opened a ballet studio in Paris to fill her lonely
hours, and with the aid of two assistants was instructing
thirty-six pupils between the ages of five and ten.

Asked to go to the last day of her life and tell us how she
was feeling, her voice sounded dispirited as she replied,
"Tired. Heartsick. Grieving. My son . . . the war . . . he
was killed . . . fighting . . . in France." She said that he had
been a lieutenant, and that word of his death had reached her
only the week before. Identifying the year as 1914, she continued, "I was sick before. Now I don't want to live." Under
questioning, she said that she had lost all of her possessions:
"My jewels, everything, the house in the Riviera; it isn't there
anymore. It was looted . . . burned." She said that she had
contracted tuberculosis while helping in a hospital, and was
now in a small French village. "One of my old servants, my
personal maid, is taking care of me," she added.

Told that the spirit had left the body, her voice seemed
tinged with awe as she whispered, "It's so beautiful . . . all
light . . . white . . . so bright." Asked to look at her former
body and describe what she saw, she said, "It's so emaciated.
The hair is all white." She later said that the body was cre-
mated, and the ashes put in a can by the sea. "That was all,"
she said simply. "Just put in a can on the beach. They were
washed out to sea."

Surprised, the hypnotist asked if she liked that disposal of
her body, and she replied, "Yes, I do. That's how my husband went, you know. In the sea." She said that she had been
happily reunited with her husband, that she recognized him
"by personality," and that their love was "still beautiful."

"Now I'm gathering my thoughts, and looking back to see
what I have to learn," she continued serenely. "That was a
beautiful life. I learned about love, but there's more to it than
I thought. I learned that you must love the God part of all
men. I loved my husband so much, and my son, that I
thought there wasn't anything else. But I learned through the
servant, who gave me all of her devotion, that you don't just

love your family, or children. You must learn to love and reach out to everyone. That is truly the way . . . as Jesus meant it to be." Told that she was now preparing to be re-born as Bertha Jennings, she said that she was selecting her parents in order to "learn humility."

"But you seem to have been a very good person in your last lifetime," the hypnotist said.

"Too much pride!" she exclaimed.

"How will you learn humility by choosing these parents?"

"By being poor. Learning to do without."

"Why have you chosen to be female again?"

"Because of the father I have chosen. The father-daughter relationship, you know. He is all love. He knows how to broadcast it. He will teach me how to love."

The hypnotist then asked Bertha to describe her birth scene and tell what was happening. "It's very fast," she began. "No trouble. There's Mrs. Green. The doctor is hand-ing me to her. She's assisting him. Now she's giving me to my father. He's wrapping me in a blanket and he says, 'It's a girl.' He sounds pleased." Asked about her mother, she said, "She's tired. She's glad it's over. She has two long braids." Asked to identify the doctor, she replied, "Dr. Kise."

After being brought back to consciousness, Bertha was mystified by the description that she had given of her birth. She said that her mother, perhaps because of Victorian reti-cence, had never discussed any of her deliveries with her, and could not even tell her the hour of her birth, when she had once sought that information for a horoscope reading. Thus, she had no idea who was present, who had delivered her, or where she was born. She puzzled about it for several hours, and then telephoned her mother long-distance. Careful to ask no leading questions, she inquired whether her father had been present at her birth, and Mrs. Jennings replied, "Cer-tainly he was there. It was nighttime, at home." Asked if it was a difficult birth, she said, "No, you came very quickly, the easiest of my children."

"Did a doctor deliver me?" Bertha prodded.

"Yes, Dr. Kise."

"Was anyone else in the room?"

"Yes. Mrs. Green and Lyle Trezora helped."

Bertha was so astonished at this ready confirmation of a scene which she could not have consciously recalled that, the next day, she volunteered to be hypnotized again. This time, after being told to go back to an earlier life and tell what was happening, she began, "Snow. I'm skiing. I'm not very good at it. I'm only twelve." She identified herself as Maria Swenson of Stockholm, but said she was on school vacation in the mountains with "Uncle Chris" Swenson. When asked what she was wearing, she said, "Earmuffs. A scarf around my neck. I have on a warm jacket. It's brown, not very pretty. My hair's a mousy color." She said that her father was a banker in Stockholm, and that she had an older and a younger sister.

Moved ahead to the age of seventeen, she gave the year as 1720, and said that her parents were killed two years previously in a bobsledding accident. Sounding disconsolate, she continued, "I'm living on this farm with Uncle Chris and his fat wife. She doesn't like me. I have to work all the time." Asked if she had inherited money from her parents, she said that it would not come to her until she was of legal age. She added that her older sister was now married, and the younger sister lived with another Swenson uncle.

She seemed so gloomy that the hypnotist moved her ahead to the age of twenty-five, hoping to find her happily married, but Maria said that she was still living on the same farm. "I work hard," she complained. "I'm always working . . . my hands look it. I'm not very attractive, you know." She said that she was not married, and had no suitors. "No chance to meet anybody in this place, and we never go anywhere." Asked if she went to church on Sundays, she sighed, "Yes, that's all. It's a little tiny country church. Lutheran."

Taken to age forty, she said that she was keeping house for her uncle since his wife's death. "She never gave anybody any peace," she muttered rebelliously. "She was a nagger." Asked if her uncle missed his wife, she exclaimed, "Oh, no! He stayed outside all the time. He's old now. I cook; keep the place clean." Queried about her inheritance from her parents, she said wearily, "It's still in the bank. I can't spend it. There's no place to spend it." The hypnotist suggested that she might buy clothes, or get her hair fixed, but she groused, "It's too late. I'm always in a big apron, or bending over something in that garden. My back hurts."

The hypnotist took her forward to the last day of that life and asked how she felt. "Tired," she groaned. She said that her uncle had been dead ten years, and had left her what he had, but she had no interest in spending money. "I'm tired. I just want to go." On being told that the soul had left the body and that she could describe her death and funeral, she said the end came quickly, after she had suffered pains in her chest. "The body is on a cot . . . in the dining room," she said. "A neighbor found it when she came to borrow something. The door was always open. We never locked doors. She went for help." She said the body was placed in a wooden box, and after a short service at the little Lutheran church, it was "put in a hole" in the churchyard. "There's almost nobody there," she said, sighing. "My, but that was a far-out place."

Asked what she had learned in that life, she said, "I was very ugly. I can't see any purpose in that life at all." Queried about the kind of life she wanted next time, she replied, "Just the opposite. Gay and pretty. I'd like to be a kinder person than my uncle's wife. I wasn't very talkative. I was resentful. I'll have to learn not to be."

Bertha was then told to go to another physical life that she would like to relive. At the end of the countdown, when asked where she was, she whispered, "Church. I'm a nun. I'm with the rest of the sisters." In answer to a series of questions, she said that she was twenty-two years old, her real name was Margaret Handel, but she was now called Sister Mary Joseph. The year was 1662, the place was Heidelberg in Germany, and her order was a nursing one. She had wanted to be a nun for as long as she could remember, and although her parents had tried to discourage her by "giving me material things," she entered at the age of eighteen.

Told to describe her appearance, she said, "I have blue eyes. Bond hair—not a very light blond. A very aristocratic nose. That's the only way I can describe it." Asked if she was considered pretty, she smilingly replied, "Angelic-looking. Sweet-looking." Had she a boy friend before entering the convent? "Only one. He still hasn't married. But it was more of a deep friendship. Eventually it might have developed into marriage if I hadn't become a nun, but he knew that I always intended to go into the convent."

Taken ahead to the age of fifty, she said that she was now a superior who oversaw other nuns in her nursing order, and that previously she too had been a nurse in a mental hospital. Asked to tell about her most difficult case, she said, "I was attacked. I was being disobedient. I thought there were things I could handle myself. I learned many, many sad lessons."

Then she began to chuckle, and on being asked to explain why she was amused, she continued to chuckle for some time before responding, "I shouldn't be laughing, I was so scared. I thought I had the patients under control, but a patient had me under control. It was a woman. She tried to kill me. My neck. She was choking me." Asked how she escaped, she replied, "She tripped. I rang the alarm, ran outside, and locked the door. I got punished for that. I was sent to a smaller hospital to learn obedience. I was so willful, I never thought I'd make it." Flashing a beautiful smile, she continued, "To be a good nun means strict obedience, but I was trying my own little methods with the patients, which I wasn't supposed to do. One learns. I had so many lessons to learn."

While tape-recording this session, I wondered if Bertha had been influenced by *A Nun's Story* in describing this somewhat similar episode; but when I afterward asked her about it, she said that she had never read the book, and could not remember having seen the motion picture made from it.

The hypnotist meanwhile moved Sister Mary Joseph forward to the last day of her life, and asked how she felt. Since a hypnotic subject ordinarily replies "tired," or "sick" in answer to that question, we were surprised when she said, "Good! It's a bustling day today. The parents are here. The parents of the sweet young things who have come in as novices. There's much confusion. I'm running around." Bertha Hahn even had the mien and physical appearance of a happy, contented sister superior as she talked, but when the hypnotist asked her to go to the very end of that life, the joyous mood vanished as she began, "Those steps . . . the stairway. I tripped. I'm falling. Oh, my head hurts. I hit my head; oh, my head, my head, oooooooh, my head!"

By now she was grasping a spot on the back of her head, and obviously suffering acutely; so the hypnotist quickly told her, "The spirit has left the body. You will feel absolutely no pain. No pain at all anymore. Look back now, and tell us what happens next."

"It's so sad," she sighed. "They're crying, and I don't like those tears. They're picking up the body. This is unfortunate!"

Asked to explain why it was "unfortunate," she replied, "It's the day the novices came. It was a day of happiness, and then this had to happen."

She said that she was fifty-four years old at the time of her death; and when the hypnotist, remarking on her good life, asked if she had had to learn any lesson from it, she smilingly replied, "Obedience! I wasn't that good! I wasn't evil, but I was a very headstrong gal. I had to learn many lessons. I learned to overcome willfulness, and not always to be a clown. When I clowned, I had to scrub floors. Prostrate myself on the floor, and confess in front of all the sisters. And I had to write it in a little book each day."

Moved ahead in the "between-lives" state to tell what she was doing, she said, "Helping others. Many need help. We all need help—to help each other. There are so many ways to help. Whatever the need. Kindness and love." Asked if she was also able to contact those in physical bodies who needed help, she responded, "Yes, in meditation. When they meditate, I can reach them with my thoughts."

It seems strange that the devout nun, with her piquant sense of humor, should seemingly have been reborn only nine years later as homely little Maria Swenson, who lived a dour and friendless life. Was this the karmic role that she had assigned herself in order to learn obedience; or had she not foreseen the early loss of the prosperous parents whom she presumably selected? Maria Swenson said that she lived to be seventy years old. This would have placed her death in 1773, since she gave the date as 1720 when she was seventeen.

Pretty, successful Colette Dupré said that she was born in the Paris of 1850. Thus, that lapse of seventy-seven years would have afforded time for another earthly sojourn, inasmuch as this entity seems to reincarnate rather quickly. Bertha Jennings was born only a decade after Colette's death during World War I. Her present life has not been a particularly easy one, but she has five attractive, well-adjusted children who are devoted to her. Bertha herself projects such warmth and love that even strangers, on meeting her for the first time, have remarked on this quality. Perhaps she has, indeed, learned the difficult lessons of obedience, humility and love.

XV

Since the Beginning

ROBERT MORRISON was fourteen years old in 1963, when a high school teacher in Midland, Texas, remarked to his mother, "Bobby is the living image of King Tutankhamen. I've been doing research on that Egyptian period, and I'm struck by the likeness." It was a comment that Mrs. Roberta Mueller and her son were to hear several times during subsequent years, and when a Philadelphia psychic later gave a life reading for him, she also identified him as the Egyptian pharaoh who had lived three thousand years ago.

Whether or not Bob Morrison is the reincarnation of the youthful ruler, whose richly endowed tomb has dazzled the world since its discovery in 1923, cannot be known; but like Tutankhamen, Bob's head seems large for his slim, lithe frame. Both sets of lips are full and sensuous, the ears thick and wide-set, the nose slightly flattened along the bridge, and the cheekbones high. In addition, Bob's eyes seem as mysterious as the curse which plagued discoverers of Tutankhamen's burial site in the Valley of the Kings at Thebes. They have a constantly changing hue, like a chameleon; and when a clerk was filling out the form for Bob's driver's license, he twice erased the notation on eye color, as his iris seemingly changed from blue to green to gray.

Robert Morrison was born in Memphis, Tennessee, which

was named for the fabled city of ancient Egypt. He spent his boyhood in Midland, and at an age when he could scarcely have heard of Shakespeare, he puzzled his mother by wandering from room to room, intoning, "O Romeo, Romeo, wherefore art thou, Romeo?" When asked where he had learned the famous lines, he could provide no logical answer.

As he entered his teens, Bob described to Mrs. Mueller a recurring dream in which he relived the death of a Roman soldier, and when his English teacher assigned her pupils to write a theme on what each considered to be the most permanent thing in life, Bob wrote that it was life itself, through reincarnation. During the years that he was dreaming of a Roman battlefield, his mother also had a recurrent dream in which she saw the same winding, tree-lined roadway. In her waking state she could not identify it, but in sleep she felt a deep sense of belonging there. One summer, during an automobile trip North, she suddenly startled her dozing son by exclaiming, "Bobby, this is it! This is the identical roadway that I've so often seen in my sleep." The lad glanced out the window, and read a signpost. They were on Shore Drive in Virginia Beach, Virginia.

Moved by inner promptings, they decided to settle in that community; and although Edgar Cayce was no longer living, Mrs. Mueller became interested enough in reincarnation to request life readings for herself and her son with Helen-Muriel Travis of Drexel Hill, Pennsylvania. The psychic first told Bob of a lifetime in Atlantis, when he was "trained for kingship in the temple," and then of a brief rulership in Egypt as the young king who died at eighteen. She next described his life as a "follower of Constantine," the first Christian emperor of Rome, saying, "You taught him spiritual knowledge that he needed to know. You were a warrior. You didn't like war, but knew that it was good to bring order, and that by conquering nations that had deteriorated, temporal order could be brought. You were very powerful physically, performing great deeds of valor; but when in Rome you loved to participate in discourses on politics, government, statesmanship, medicine, the arts, and especially architecture. You helped to plan and build aqueducts, roads, arches, coliseums, houses, and baths." She said that his death was "instantaneous," and although she did not elaborate, this could have been the one he had experienced in his dreams.

Miss Travis further described an Egyptian reincarnation in

which Robert Morrison was said to have been a merchant-trader who sailed his ships down the Nile and across the Mediterranean, "through the Pillars of Hercules," to the southern shores of Britain, where he exchanged enamels and gems, ivory-inlaid furniture and hand-wrought jewelry for tin. Although prosperous and well-liked, the merchant had incurred the enmity of the priesthood by refusing to take sacrifices to the temple. He believed that the priests were "exploiting the people and stealing from the throne itself," and because he refused to be a party to their chicanery, the priests forbade other Egyptians to trade with him. Artisans were ordered to sell to him only at exorbitant prices, or risk expulsion from the Temple; and his neighbors were instructed to turn wild beasts loose on his property, to despoil the house and grounds.

At last the merchant appealed to the king, but the ruler replied that he was powerless to mediate a dispute with the priests, "because they have more rice, more wealth and more troops than I have." The entranced psychic said this hurt the merchant so deeply "in a spiritual sense that there was an instant break in the brain above the right eye—a karmic debt that you owed for having despondently taken your own life, as an Inca, in Peru. Paralyzed, you could neither speak nor move. They sent for your junior partner, who is your mother in this lifetime, and he cared for you until you soon passed over."

Two other lifetimes were detailed by Miss Travis. In one, she said that Bob Morrison was a temple dancer in Cambodia; a beautiful, delicate child named Krishna whose parents had pledged her to the temple, with the stipulation that on reaching marriageable age she would be permitted to leave if her intended husband was able to repay the temple in gold for her lost services. One evening, a sixteen-year-old nobleman in attendance at a temple feast saw the beautiful little dancer, and fell in love with her. He assumed that the twelve-year-old child was pledged for life to the temple, but his father asked the boy's mother to make a retreat there in order to learn more about the girl. The mother also came to love the "adorable being," and experienced "great joy" when the chief priest said that Krishna could marry if she chose. That evening the priest summoned Krishna, told her that a young man from a wealthy, spiritual family had fallen in love with her, and suggested that she meditate three days before reaching a decision.

The first night, after preparing herself by ritual, she had a vision of the high priest praying for her enlightenment. The seond night her vision was of the mother of the boy, holding out her arms and saying that if she married her son, she would be treated with love and gentleness the rest of her life. The third night's vision was of the boy, reaching out his hand and vowing to treat her as his bride "all of my days." The girl then arose, went to the high priest, and said that she wished to "go to my husband when the time is arrived." The young nobleman's mother was identified as Bob Morrison's own mother in the present lifetime, and Mrs. Mueller considers it more than coincidental that, if Robert had been a girl in this lifetime, she had planned to name the baby Kristina.

Helen-Muriel Travis said the Cambodian marriage was such a blissfully happy one that "when the entity now known as Robert Morrison" next incarnated as a male in Elizabethan England, he subconsciously "felt a reluctance to be masculine again." She said his surname in that lifetime was Spenser, and that he gradually freed himself from the strong attachment to the Cambodian incarnation by playing feminine roles in Shakespearean plays.

"You become a happy, successful actor," she told him, "and I can hear you calling, 'O, Romeo, Romeo, wherefore art thou, Romeo.' But your father wanted you to complete your education, and as the memory of your feminine lifetime faded, you went back to school. After graduation you went to Court, where your illusions of women were shattered. You were shocked by their wiles as they pursued you, and by the greed, the drinking, and the disloyalty of the courtesans. Your family owned several estates, both in London and in the country, and you went into local politics. You worked for the throne, but because of the easy virtue of the women at Court, you did not consider marriage until you were forty. Then, at the home of a squire in a small manor house on your estate you met his daughter Elsbeth, who was only sixteen, but emotionally mature. You quickly became engaged, and your marriage was very happy. As time passed you had sons and daughters. You had dogs, horses, cats, and deer in the park.

"You had great love for everything aesthetic, and because

of a carry-over from the Roman life you were drawn many times to Italy, bringing back ancient statues, paintings and other objets d'art. You designed your English house in the neoclassic Roman style that you had favored when an amateur architect in the Roman life, and you and your young wife surrounded yourselves with poetry and music. You personally knew William Shakespeare, and although you seem not to have been the poet Spenser [Edmund Spenser who wrote *The Faerie Queene*] you were of that family."

Although it is impossible to prove whether any of these life readings are factual, it seems rather significant that the psychic not only linked Bob Morrison with Egyptian rulership and life as a Roman soldier, but also "heard" him repeating Juliet's famous lines about Romeo which had so engrossed him as a child.

Bob Morrison was fifteen years old at the time of the reading, and he has not since dreamed of death as a Roman soldier, but at the age of eighteen he may have glimpsed a fragment of his most recent previous lifetime. In reality, he had been introduced to an older man whose friendship could have opened doors for him, but the man reacted almost violently to him, exclaiming to others, "He looks like a left-over from the Bolshevik Revolution." Several months later, Bob had a vivid dream in which he was dressed in mufti, with a red kerchief tied around his neck. He knew that he was a participant in the Russian Revolution, one of a group under orders to enter government buildings and arrest the officials. When an ornate door failed to open he broke it down, and with gun drawn, entered the office. There, behind the desk, was the man he had met three months before in Virginia Beach, and he later told his mother, "I couldn't kill him. I couldn't make myself pull the trigger, but the man grabbed a pistol from the drawer of his desk and blew out his brains. I saw the brains spill all over his desk and the floor. It was such a gruesome sight that I awakened in a state of shock, and couldn't go back to sleep."

Could the dream have been simply a carry-over of the man's unkind remark about his resemblance to the Bolsheviks, or had the older man subconsciously recognized the young revolutionist who once caused him to take his life? We may never know, but in an earlier dream Bob had seemed to see the ending of that lifetime, when as a Russian saboteur he was captured by German Nazis, and eventually hung. True it is that in this lifetime he has a virtual obsession about not wearing a necktie, preferring his throat to be free of encumbrance.

There is no question but that Robert Morrison has remarkably vivid dreams, of a type which Edgar Cayce had indicated could be past-life memories. Recently, after briefly meeting an older couple for the first time, he dreamed the same night that a man in a flowing robe spoke to him of the couple, saying, "They were Robert and Elizabeth Barrett Browning in their previous lifetime, and you were associated with them." Bob says that he has seen this same berobed figure many times in his dreams, and invariably feels great respect for him. This would indicate, according to Edgar Cayce's teachings, that the figure is Morrison's own higher self, or superconscious.

There is an interesting aftermath to this incident. Roberta Mueller subsequently mentioned to the couple that her son had dreamed of them, but all that she disclosed concerning it was this: "He was told that you were a rather well-known English couple in the nineteenth century."

Inasmuch as I was present during this encounter, I can testify to the fact that the older woman exclaimed, "Don't tell me that we were the Brownings!" She then seemed overcome by embarrassment at having spontaneously uttered such an immodest statement, since the thought of having been a famous English poetess had never before entered her mind. This could, of course have been mental telepathy, but more surprises were yet to come. Mrs. Mueller, commenting on the fact that Robert Browning and the woman's husband shared the same given name, laughingly remarked that it would be "just too much" if the woman's middle name were Elizabeth. It was not; but strangely enough her mother had settled on the name of Elizabeth for her, until the baby's father objected so strenuously to "Elizabeth" that it was changed. This has since been verified to me by her mother.

There were also other coincidences. The woman majored in poetry at Baylor University in Texas, which has the largest Robert Browning collection in the world. For much of her life, Elizabeth Barrett Browning suffered from a spinal affliction; her favorite country, aside from her homeland, was Italy; and she became vitally interested in contact between the living and the so-called dead, to the consternation of Robert Browning, who did not believe in it. These facts are equally true of the woman whom Bob Morrison saw in his dream; yet neither he nor his mother was aware of such parallels, since they had barely met the couple, and were also unfamiliar with the lives of the Brownings.

In March of 1968, Robert Morrison submitted for the first time to hypnosis, and when told to go "back back back in time" until he occupied another body, he said that he was an Indian in South America, serving as a guide in the desert, and that it was sundown. Asked to describe what he was doing, he said that he was wrapping himself in a blanket and preparing to sleep behind a big rock. Moved ahead two years and asked the date, he replied, "I think it's fifteen hundred something, but we don't number the years." In response to further questions, he said that he was standing on a high mountain looking at some old Indian ruins which his ancestors had built; that he lived there when not traveling as a guide, and had no wife or family.

When the hypnotist took him forward to the last day of that life and asked how he felt, he muttered, "Depressed. I'm much older. I'm not sick," and added that he was now inside the ruins which he had previously described from the exterior. "There's a carving of a sunburst on the wall," he continued. "I glanced at it just now as I walked past. I'm looking at the treasure here—just kicking it around. It's in an underground room of the ruins." He identified the treasure as "mostly gold," but when asked if he meant gold coins, he corrected, "Not coins. Gold weapons, knives. . . ." Asked again for the date, he replied, "We don't have a year."

A little later he said that he was walking with a friend, and carrying a gold sacrificial knife in his hand. "It's not the right one, though," he volunteered. "I was hunting for another one, but there's so much treasure I couldn't find it." Of his friend, he said, "He's one of my race, but he's part Spaniard. He's afraid of me." Asked if that was because of his knife, he replied in the negative, saying, "He respects me. My ancestors were royalty. That's why he fears me."

Told to spell out his own name, he replied, "I don't believe our language is written. We don't have an alphabet." Pressed to tell what others called him, he said it sounded "something like eagle or eela," and that his tribe's name was the same.

Told to go forward several hours, he suddenly announced, "I'm going to kill myself. I don't want to, but I'm the last of my race, and I'm all alone. My friend is gone now. I'm mad at him because he's a half-breed, and I don't want to do the same thing." He explained that the reason why he had not married was because no pure stock of his lineage remained, and his parents were long dead. He said that he was still on the mountain, from which vantage point he could see the desert far below. Asked to tell what he was doing, he said, "Nothing. I wait for the sun to go down. I will kill myself just as it goes down." The hypnotist tried to argue him out of suicide, to no avail; then counted to five, told him that the sun had set, and asked what happened.

"I stabbed myself," the subject said wearily. "Below the heart, I think. But I'm not dead. There's just a lot of blood. I'm getting weaker. The sun is gone, but the moon is not yet up." Told that the spirit had left the body, and that he could now describe the death scene without pain, he declared, "My body is on a cliff, fallen across a large boulder. I'm lying on my stomach, crumpled up. The knife is in me." Asked to tell what lesson he had learned in that life, he replied, "Greed. The reason I killed myself was greed. Someone tried to force me to draw a map that would lead him to the treasure. People knew I knew where it was, but it didn't belong to them. I sealed the entrance to the room before I died, but there were many other places where treasure was hidden. I wasn't greedy. I learned that others were."

When moved ahead and questioned about the purpose of that life, he indicated that he had assessed it more thoroughly, because this time he said, "I didn't think my lesson was learned well enough. I think I was also greedy in that life. I tried to sell some of the treasure of my ancestors in a town, and that's when the trouble started. A lot of men were trying to find it, and they knew that I knew the location."

After being brought back to consciousness, Bob exclaimed in surprise, "I was actually in that body. I could feel the emotions as if they were mine, but I can't figure out where all that stuff came from." His mother reminded him that the woman psychic, in the life reading for him several years before, had briefly mentioned that in an Inca incarnation he had taken his life, but he said that he did not consciously remember that.

The three of us thereupon set to work to research the Incas. We learned that the culture had thrived in the mountains and deserts of Peru and neighboring areas until 1533,

when Francisco Pizarro, a Spaniard, treacherously imprisoned Atahualpa, the last Inca ruler, after luring him to a con-
clave. Atahualpa declined to be converted to Christianity or
to accept Spanish sovereignty, but agreed to pay a ransom of
four million dollars in gold and silver bullion. The wily Pizarro collected the vast hoard, but continued to hold him
prisoner, knowing that much more treasure was hidden. He
finally killed Atahualpa, after charging that he was conspir-
ing to overthrow his Spanish conquerors, and that he had
given secret orders for the assassination of his half brother
Huascar.

If Bob Morrison was actually the last of the Inca royal
line, he was probably descended from the murdered Huascar,
who inherited the Inca throne from his father because he was
of pure line, and Atahualpa was not. *The Encyclopaedia Britannica* states that the latter, who usurped the throne from
his half brother, was considered illegitimate by Peruvian law
because his mother was the daughter of the conquered sover-
eign of Quito, and therefore "was not descended on both
sides from the line of the Incas." This fact could have explained Bob Morrison's resentment toward his friend because
he was "a half-breed," and his own unwillingness to marry
outside the royal line.

Our research further disclosed that the Incas, unlike some
neighboring tribes, had no system of writing, or a calendar;
and that they chiefly worshipped the sun, from whom Inca
rulers were considered to be directly descended. Bob Morrison had pointedly mentioned the sunburst carved on the wall
of the treasure room, and had stressed that he must wait to
die until the sun went down. We also learned that Inca rulers
were simply called The Inca by their people, and Bob had
said that he was called by the same name as his tribe. If Bob
had been trying to fake the role, he would surely have identified himself as an Inca. Instead, he said that the name
sounded "something like eagle or eela." We do not, of course,
know how the Incas pronounced the name of their tribe four
hundred years ago; but I made an interesting discovery several weeks later, while reading an advance copy of Edgar
Evans Cayce's since-published book about his father, *Edgar
Cayce On Atlantis*. In a reading given in 1933, which described the scattering of Atlanteans to Europe, Egypt and
South America when their own continent was breaking up,
Cayce spoke of "that peoples called the Incal . . . in the Pe-

ruvian land." Incal does indeed sound "something like eagle or eela," although Bob Morrison had never heard the word before; and he could not have been picking it from our minds telepathically, since it was also unknown to any of us present when he was hypnotized.

An eminent geologist who is convinced of reincarnation has said of hypnotic regression, "This is the way that we should study history. It could be of immeasurable assistance in learning more about ancient geological times, as well as little-known periods in the development of mankind."

If the material which emerges from the subconscious mind of a hypnotized subject is as authentic about previous lives as it has proved to be in uncovering forgotten memories of the present life, even to the birth scene, it would indeed enrich our knowledge of the earth, its peoples, and obscure events. Certainly the sad ending of a proud line of Indian nobles, as described by Bob Morrison, and the happy but fearful cave life depicted by Vickey Hinchman, in the remote past when the Arctic Circle was tropical, are currently to be found in no history books.

Bob's mother, Mrs. Roberta Mueller, was born in Pretoria, South Africa, in 1924, the daughter of Johannes Frederick Theobaldt Mostert, a sugar planter, and his wife. Roberta's ancestors were among the first Dutch settlers, having gone to South Africa with the Dutch East Indies Company in 1652; and her grandfather, Andrew M. Mostert, became one of that country's first millionaires, owning large plantations and also recruiting labor for the diamond mines. Johannes was called Theo, and when he was ready for college his father sent him to Kansas State University, where he fell in love with a coed from Arkansas. After graduation, Theo and his American bride went to South Africa for three years, and then settled in Arkansas, where they published a newspaper. In her late teens, Roberta enrolled in the journalism school at the University of Missouri, but married before graduation. Her mother is now dead, and her father is living in Johannesburg, South Africa.

From earliest childhood, Roberta has been interested in herbs, which she collected in the woods near her Arkansas home. Following her move to Virginia Beach in 1964, she awakened one Sunday morning with excruciating gout pains, and because her physician was unavailable, she began drinking quantities of saffron herb tea. The swelling shortly disappeared, and when she later told her doctor what she had done, he recommended that she continue the treatment, inasmuch as colchicine (the standard medical remedy for gout, which is a derivative of saffron) sometimes has unpleasant side effects.

On Christmas morning, Mrs. Mueller had a vision of a friend crying with pain while her husband bent over the bed, helplessly trying to comfort her, and she inwardly heard the words, "It is her kidneys." Roberta immediately telephoned to ask what was wrong with Clara, and learned that she had correctly envisioned the bedside scene. Clara was suffering from sharp back pains, and since Roberta had psychically diagnosed the trouble as uric acid from a kidney infection, she rushed over with a supply of saffron tea. After returning home, she "saw" Clara drinking a cup and falling asleep; awakening and asking for more, then peacefully sleeping again. The next day the friend called Roberta to thank her, and reported that after two cups of the tea she had "slept the clock around." Her pain was gone.

Another time, Mrs. Mueller learned that a friend had a chronic case of diarrhea which doctors had been unsuccessfully treating for several years. She recommended a tea brewed from the leaves of raspberry, strawberry and comfrey leaves, with the addition of peppermint, and the friend has had no further discomfort.

Roberta Mueller's interest in herbs was totally unknown to Helen-Muriel Travis of Pennsylvania, but when the psychic gave life readings for Bob and his mother the following year, she told Roberta of a Greek incarnation "at the time of Artaxerxes when you were a healer-priest, who brought your healing knowledge with you from a much earlier lifetime."

She then described an Atlantean incarnation, in a setting abounding with wild turkeys, where Roberta was said to have been Am Om Phares, a boy of ten who was "a child of nature." She saw the lad lovingly selecting roots, leaves, bark and plants, and meditating on them to acquire knowledge of their uses. From them he made ointments, poultices and medicines which not only effected cures for the physical body, but improved the psychic senses of sight, hearing, taste and smell. She said that Am Om regularly carried his medicines to the temple in two little hand-woven baskets, offering one as a sacrifice, and having the other blessed by the priests.

Atlanteans reportedly came from all parts of the continent

to receive treatment, "walking in as physical and emotional wrecks, and walking out whole"; and soon a temple garden was "consecrated to Am Om's use, as a laboratory for his work with herbs." The psychic described Am Om in his prime as nearly six feet tall, with "rosy copper skin, wide-open dark eyes, a compassionate mouth, high cheekbones, and long silky dark hair on which you wore a golden circlet studded with gems, which represented wisdom and healing." She added that he lived "several centuries, as men were meant to live," and that one night his soul peacefully left his body, although it was free from pain or disease. The body then lay in state from sunrise to sunset in the temple, while sacred dances were performed by the priesthood.

Naturally it is impossible to verify an account of a prehistoric life, on a continent of whose existence we lack proof, but it seems remarkable that Miss Travis pinpointed an occupation then which is Mrs. Mueller's abiding hobby in this lifetime; for she stocks a cupboard with some forty different herbs, and blends them into healing combinations for family and friends.

Among the more disheartening aspects of research in the field of reincarnation is, of course, the difficulty of checking out the alleged facts. During that same life reading, Roberta Mueller was told of another lifetime as a Quaker lass in Benjamin Franklin's day. Her name was said to have been Deborah Ruth Thompson, or Tomkins, and she was born in 1769 on what is now Green Street in Philadelphia. The three-story house was connected with her father's store, where he sold candles, trinkets, lanterns, farming equipment and furniture, some of them imported from abroad. Deborah was depicted as a devout, but gay and popular girl, who after her marriage to Thornton Simpson moved to West Virginia, where her husband broke the ground, built their house, traded with Indians, and shipped produce by flatboat. A great deal of detail was given about her life there and in Philadelphia, but when Vivian H. Newlin was kind enough to check records at the Friends' Historical Library in Swarthmore College and the Historical Society of Pennsylvania, no proof was forthcoming. Mrs. Newlin located a Thomas Thompson who was born in 1747, the same year that the psychic had given as the date of Deborah's father's birth, but none of his six children had the name Deborah Ruth. She found a Deborah Thompson who was born in 1765, but that was her married name. The nearest that she could come to Thornton Simpson was a Thomas Simpson of that period.

Similarly disappointing from a factual viewpoint was a life reading given for me by a New York psychic, who described a number of interesting lifetimes in Egypt, Palestine, India and France, and said that in the early nineteenth century, I was the daughter of a Quaker minister who was the namesake of the famous New England preacher, Jonathan Edwards. She said that Bertha Hahn of Newark, Delaware, was then my sister, and that our home was in Ephrata, Pennsylvania. Our names were said to be Wilma and Willene Edwards, and a brother was named William Edwards. The reading declared that we lost our mother while in our teens, and that we later became teachers and counselors, but Mrs. Newlin was unable to verify that such a Quaker family had existed in that era. Although the lack of records does not conclusively prove the nonexistence of such a family, it is nevertheless disconcerting to find no trace of it a hundred and fifty years later.

Proof of identity is also lacking when more prominent names emerge from the past. Edgar Cayce told Riley Simmons, a Norfolk insurance executive, that in one of his recent incarnations he had been General Israel Putnam, of Revolutionary War fame; and although the reading supplied a great deal of detail which checked out with historical accuracy, as well as some which would supplement the history of that era, it is impossible to prove or disprove that the general who died in 1790 is now reincarnated. The seer's assertion that Simmons' wife, Beverly, was once Leila Beverly Cayce is somewhat more evidential, in that she was born on the thirty-fourth anniversary of Leila's death and bears a remarkable physical resemblance to another of Cayce's sisters; but cynics can reasonably argue that Cayce may have been subconsciously influenced by that look-alike quality in assigning Beverly the role of Leila.

Investigators have had far greater success with verifying places and names in instances of spontaneous childhood recall, perhaps because the lives that the youngsters claim to have lived were of such recent date that the alleged relatives and friends are still living. Dr. Ian Stevenson of Charlottesville, Virginia, has researched many such claims besides those detailed in *Twenty Cases Suggestive of Reincarnation,* and has found some remarkable substantiation. Of the more than six hundred cases in his file, about half occurred in Southeast Asia, and only a few in the United States and Canada. A possible explanation for the preponderance of Oriental cases is the fact that Eastern religions embrace the doctrine of reincarnation, whereas an American toddler who prattled about a previous lifetime would probably be chastised and told to stop imagining things.

Hinduism is the oldest surviving religion in the world today, and since its followers believe in the cycle of rebirth, it is not surprising that we hear of children like Shanti Devi from time to time in India. Dr. Stevenson, after personal investigation of numerous cases there, declared, "The case usually starts when a small child of two to four years begins talking to his parents or siblings of a life he led in another time and place. The child usually feels a considerable pull back toward the events of that life and he frequently importunes his parents to let him return to the community where he claims that he formerly lived. If the child makes enough particular statements about the previous life, the parents (usually reluctantly) begin inquiries about their accuracy."

One of the youngsters about whom Dr. Stevenson reports is Sukla, daughter of Sri K. N. Sen Gupta of the village of Kampa, West Bengal, who was born in 1954. When barely able to talk, she began cradling a block of wood or a pillow, and calling it Minu. When asked who Minu was, Sukla replied that she was her daughter. During the next three years she revealed additional information about Minu, as well as her "husband" and his younger brothers, Khetu and Kartuna. She claimed that they lived at Rathtala in Bhatpara, and although her parents knew of Bhatpara, they had never heard of Rathtala, or of the people whom Sukla mentioned.

The child pleaded so insistently that her father mentioned the problem to a fellow employee of a railroad, who offered to check with his relatives in Bhatpara. He subsequently reported that a man named Khetu, who lived in a section called Rathtala, had in 1948 lost a sister-in-law who left an infant girl named Minu. Sukla's parents therefore took her to Bhatpara and Rathtala, where she led them to the house of her alleged father-in-law, Sri Amritalal Chakravarty. She correctly identified a number of people and objects, and her meeting with the supposed former husband and daughter so deeply aroused her emotions that she thereafter pined for them, between visits. Although Minu was now considerably taller than five-year-old Sukla, the latter lavished on her maternal affection such as she exhibited for no one else. Whenever she heard that Minu was ill she wept, and once became so distraught that her family had to take her to Minu's bedside. At the age of three, according to her father, Sukla had avoided eating with her brothers and sisters, saying, "Why should I eat with you? I am a Brahmin." When they eventually met her "former family," they learned that the Chakravartys are Brahmins, whereas the Guptas are not.

Another Stevenson-investigated case is that of Parmod Sharma, son of Professor Bankey Lal Sharma, who was born in Bisauli, Uttar Pradesh, India, on October 11, 1944. At the age of two and a half he told his mother not to cook, because he had a wife in Moradabad who could perform that chore. A little later, he began to talk of a large soda and biscuit shop in Moradabad, and another in Saharanpur, which he claimed to have operated under the name Mohan Brothers. He supplied many other details about the family, exhibited remarkable knowledge of biscuit making, and said that he died from eating too much curd.

His parents ignored his entreaties to visit Moradabad, but through others word reached the Mehra family, who owned a soda and biscuit shop called Mohan Brothers there and in Saharanpur. Curious, several members of that family journeyed to Bisauli to meet the lad, but found Parmod away. Later, Parmod accompanied his father and a cousin to Moradabad and Saharanpur, where he recognized several family members by name, correctly told how his desk used to be placed in the shop, and identified buildings in both towns. The Mehra family verified that Parmanand Mehra had died in 1943 of a gastrointestinal illness and appendicitis, after gorging himself on curd, seventeen months before Parmod was born. The brothers also confirmed that Parmanand had been the founder and manager of the family business before his death, and that as claimed by five-year-old Parmod, Parmanand left a wife, four sons and a daughter.

Judging by the material transmitted through spontaneous recall, life readings, hypnosis and reverie, there is no set pattern to the lapse of time between births, or to the frequency of reincarnation. Most of those children who claimed to recall former lifetimes would have returned quickly, within one to ten years, and this may make it easier for them to recapture the details of which they speak so convincingly.

Others have seemingly delayed their rebirth for decades, or even centuries, presumably to contemplate past errors and develop spiritual understanding before plunging again into earthly temptations where new tests must be met, and old debts settled. The Cayce readings indicate that although many of us have lived thousands of times before, we seldom work on the karma incurred in more than a few of them, in any one incarnation. Thus, Cayce ordinarily detailed no more than five or six lifetimes, although those could range from "Lost Atlantis" and ancient Egypt to modern-day America.

Edgar Cayce taught that the more highly evolved souls ordinarily choose their parents and the circumstances into which they are born, although this selectivity is not necessarily available to underdeveloped, or depraved souls. Sometimes carnal desires get in the way of this selectivity. Another example is that of thousands of young men killed in wars, some of whom are so eager to return and fulfill the lives they had hopefully begun that they seize upon any available vehicle—any expectant mother—to fulfill that wish. Hugh Lynn Cayce says that sometimes they are caught in a vortex over which they can exercise no control; that having made themselves available for rebirth, they may be drawn as by a magnet into a household that is not suitable for their talents or desires.

Psychics repeatedly stress that it is therefore wise to prepare oneself, through daily meditation, for a continuation of life after death, in order to avoid the shock of one's passing; and that the way to prevent being drawn back too quickly is to free oneself of habits and desires of the ulterior type that could keep one too earthbound. An entity who is unable to curb his overindulgence in liquor or sex can carry that obsession with him beyond the grave, where the longing for it proves so irresistible that he returns almost immediately, without the philosophical preparation that could permit him to select his next incarnation with wisdom.

The moral would seem to be: Discipline yourself to become the sort of person now that you would like to be the next time around.

A logical question asked by numerous people who discount the idea of reincarnation is this: If all souls have existed since the beginning of time, how does it happen that the world population is so much greater today than at other times in history? Where do so many souls come from?

Edgar Cayce, while in the unconscious state, declared that

a population larger than that of the earth today once inhabited the lost continents of Atlantis, about which Plato wrote, and Lemuria, in the southeastern Pacific; and that after the cataclysms which inundated them, the world population was decimated. This parallels the Biblical story of the flood, after which Noah and his family had to begin again to repeople the planet. Cayce said that although no life as we know it exists on other planets in our own solar system, there are other life forms in the universe, and between earthly lives souls can continue their development in various mental planes.

The seer declared that souls who inhabited Atlantis are now returning in vast numbers, and that the continent itself will soon begin to emerge around Bimini. Inasmuch as he also prophesied that large areas of the earth's surface will disappear into the sea before the close of this century, through a shift of the axis, this would indicate that we are building up to another cataclysmic disaster such as that which presumably destroyed masses of peoples in remote times. If true, those who are alarmed about the current population explosion and resultant famine will find that particular problem to be nonexistent. The souls would be imperishable, and, according to the Cayce readings, life would continue in other planes until the earth could once again support large numbers of physical bodies.

XVI

To Know Ourselves

NEARLY every thinking adult is aware of the spiritual crisis now confronting us, and of its profound effect on behavioral patterns in America. The bloody disorders in ghettos and city streets are perhaps symptomatic of a larger problem than mere economics: the frustration which besets man when he feels impotent to chart his own destiny. Government has become so big, and the powers of destruction so engulfing, that we seem to be losing our sense of individuality, our Oneness with God. Now that giant computers can spew out the sum total of our working lives when fed our Social Security numbers, even our names seem stripped of significance, and we begin to feel like faceless cogs in an impersonally grinding wheel.

What is life and what is death? Science has made such miraculous strides in the past quarter century that it can orbit man into outer space and can probe the ocean's depths, but it cannot answer this far more vital question. Nor can satisfactory explanations be obtained in our churches, schools, or governmental think-tanks.

This gnawing search for personal identity has led many young people into dope addiction, or on illusory psychedelic trips which can be mind-shattering. The paucity of metaphysical thinking in our Western culture has sent the Beatles and others on pilgrimages to the Far East to study meditation with a yogi; and it is almost impossible to pick up a current magazine without finding an article on meditation, or on the search for one's self. Man's longing to know himself is as old as time, but perhaps never before has it engrossed the active attention of so many Westerners. This is an encouraging omen of a spiritual reawakening which seems to be thrusting aside some of the shackles of our materialistic society.

The need for self-identification is acute, for when a man fears that he is losing his personal identity with the society in which he must work and live, it is not surprising that he feels tempted to hurl bricks through plate-glass windows and join in violent uprisings. It is a way of attracting attention to the "self" that he seems to have lost. Another way is to let one's hair and beard grow long, to scorn the bath, and take narcissistic pleasure in the odor of one's body. Some seek identity through self-indulgences, but even hedonism begins to pall when the questions of life and death still await, in the sobering morning light. Today's youths may scorn their parents who work for a living, but the time comes when they too must eat, or starve. In some Eastern cultures they could don saffron robes and go about with begging bowls, but in our complicated economic structure they must work, or steal; and if apprehended for the latter they must relinquish that which they most cherish, the freedom to do as they please.

The groping of modern man for a purpose in life is by no means confined to the hippies. The so-called flower children are simply dramatizing a deep need within all of us to find an awareness of self. Who am I? Meditation is the key which unlocks this illusive door, and one need not journey to the Himalayas to seek an ashram. This "holy place" can be found in his own home, or in any quiet spot where he will be receptive and attentive.

Such Western thinkers as Dr. Carl G. Jung and Dr. Rudolf Steiner were extolling the discipline of meditation long before the birth of the Beatles or hippies; and a semiliterate Kentuckian named Edgar Cayce was teaching these same truths before he had ever heard of meditation, except through his own unconscious. No more dramatic example of reincarnation can be cited than that of Edgar Cayce himself: a man who knew nothing of medicine or metaphysics or world cultures in the waking state, but who exhibited a staggering array of knowledge on almost any subject when in self-induced trance. Either he had mastered those subjects in many previous lifetimes, or he was tapping into what Dr. Jung called the Collective Unconscious. If the latter is the total explanation, then by what means did Cayce acquire the remarkable ability to read this cosmic storehouse of knowledge, unless he had perfected that art in some previous incarnation?

Cayce taught that meditation not only deepens our self-awareness, but can lift the curtain on seemingly forgotten memories of other lives in ages past. By doing so, we can better understand our present self and our purpose. In meditation we seek to know the God part of ourselves and to feel His Presence. This is not to be confused with prayer. When we pray, we talk to God. When we meditate, we listen. Cayce once put it this way: "Ye find Him within thine own heart, within thine own consciousness. If ye will meditate, open thy heart, thy mind. Let thy body and mind be channels that ye may do the things ye ask God to do for you. Thus ye come to know Him."

At the beginning, meditation should be practiced at the same time, in the same place, for fifteen minutes each day. We should choose a quiet spot where we can await the "stillness within," and if such a spot cannot be found during the day, we can set the alarm for two A.M. The peace and quietude of that fifteen-minute interval will more than compensate for the lost sleep. Lie flat, or sit with spine erect and comfortable. Breathe rhythmically, while focusing the attention on a single object, mental image or spiritual thought. The undisciplined mind will frequently rove, but it should be snared and gently returned to the central focus. Be patient. The stillness, the light, and inner knowing may not come for months or years, but even as we despair of achieving the illumination that we seek, we are changing within—becoming more intuitive, more perceptive, more assured and aware.

If we do not observe this gradual improvement in ourselves, others will; for as we open the psychic centers for a free exchange of love between God and ourselves, we are also opening them to others. We can even learn to love ourselves, the hardest task of all, because we will come to know ourselves.

Is God dead? No, He is simply trying to awaken our slumbering selves; to tell us that all men are brothers regardless of creed, sex or color, and that what we do to others we do to ourselves. It does no good to exclaim, "After me the deluge," or "Thank heavens, I won't live to see the disaster that lies ahead"; for life is continuous, and we will probably soon find ourselves back in an earthly body, reaping the whirlwind that we have sown. If one suffers, all of us suffer, because we are a community of souls who returned together. Better then that we should unite in our search for God—the God Who is within all of us.

XVII

God Punishes No Man

THE tendency nowadays is to blame anyone except ourselves for our misfortunes. It is the fault of the parents or of modern society that youths turn to dope and crime. The reason that a man fails to succeed is that he is the product of an unfortunate environment, or a member of a downtrodden race. God was unfair to give us a defective body, or poor parents, when so many others have greater advantages.

But self-pity has no place in the philosophy of reincarnation. As a man sows, so shall he reap, and unless we live helpfully in this lifetime, making the most of our opportunities to serve, the next incarnation is likely to be more unpleasant still. Most Orientals believe that the law of karma is inexorable. If we steal in this life, our goods will be stolen from us in the next. If we kill, we too shall die by violence. There is no escape from the wheel of karma and our own misdeeds.

Perhaps Edgar Cayce's greatest contribution to the philosophy of reincarnation was his reassuring message that we have a choice; that there is a law of Grace as well as a law of karma, and that we have free will to set the path of our soul, before deciding to incarnate. Hugh Lynn Cayce, who directs the foundation which carries on his father's work, says of this teaching:

172

"We move under the law of Grace the moment that we begin to forgive ourselves and others. To forgive is divine. God has already forgiven us. How else could He have welcomed the prodigal son with open arms, had He not already forgiven him? To forgive ourself is to rid ourself of guilt. To forgive others is to rid ourselves of the resentments and hates which twist our souls and make us sick. Anger is a thought pattern, and we build karma from thought patterns as surely as from deeds. As Dad so often said, Mind is the Builder. Grace is the love of God pouring out continuously on man. We must learn to forgive quickly, never sleeping on a resentment or a quarrel. Blaming others keeps us from loving others, and prevents the law of Grace from taking over. If we can't love everybody, then we should practice on one person at a time, until we have learned the art of loving. We come under the law of Grace whenever we choose it instead of the law of karma."

Edgar Cayce said that karma is a reaction which may be compared to the reaction within the body when a piece of food is taken into the system. "The food is translated into a part of the body itself," he continued, "penetrating to every cell, and influencing the health of the body and mind. Thus it is with a soul when it enters a body for an experience on earth. The person's thoughts are the food upon which the soul feeds, along with the actions which result from these thoughts. These thoughts and actions in return have been generated by thoughts and actions behind them, and so on back to the birth of the soul. When a soul enters a new body, in a new environment, a door is opened leading to an opportunity for building the soul's destiny. Everything which has been previously built, both good and bad, is contained in that opportunity. There is always a way of redemption, but there is no way to dodge responsibilities which the soul has itself undertaken."

By this, Edgar Cayce meant that we ourselves select the pattern of our lives before we are born, and having once set that course, we cannot escape from the obligations thus assumed. Hugh Lynn Cayce said that on several different occasions, his father tried to break away from the grueling task that he had set for himself in this most recent lifetime; but that despite the heaviness of the burden, he was always forced to return to it. The burden was perhaps even heavier on Gertrude Cayce, Hugh Lynn's mother, who uncomplainingly bore the brunt of a household continually overrun with people who felt that through past-life associations with the famous seer, they had a rightful claim on his constant attention to their problems.

Hugh Lynn said that without his mother's gentle dedication to the task, his father's work could never have been brought to fruition, and she survived the husband whom she adored by only a few months. Interestingly, in a life reading which Edgar Cayce once gave for his wife, he said that the entity wavered for twenty-four hours before entering the body that she inhabited during this lifetime, because of the unusually strenuous task that she had assigned herself. Once having chosen, however, she never shirked her job.

Many Hindus seek to achieve nirvana, or emancipation from the cycle of rebirths, by withdrawing from their fellowmen and living an ascetic life of meditation and contemplation. But Grace comes with loving, forgiving, and serving others, not by withdrawing from them, and Jesus Christ gave the world a new commandment, "Love one another." We cannot truly love another if we hold grudges against him; so if we have quarreled it is important that we quickly say, "Forgive me, I'm sorry," or "I forgive you. I love you."

How many hundreds of times we have recited the Lord's Prayer by rote, without pausing to grasp the awesome meaning of the line "Forgive us our trespasses as we forgive those who trespass against us." Let us ponder the significance of the word "as." What we are actually asking God to do is to forgive us to the same degree that we forgive others. This places the burden on our own hearts. If we would have God forgive our evil thoughts and deeds, so that we can come under the law of Grace instead of the law of karma, then we must just as wholeheartedly forgive our own debtors.

To love. To forgive. Is this really so hard to do, if we remember that God also created our rival, and that He loves him as compassionately as He does us? God has already forgiven both of us. Can we not do likewise?

God punishes no man. We punish ourselves through the resentments which give us allergies, the hatreds which make us ill, and the karmic retribution that we have chosen to work out. We brought with us into this life the permanent record of our own foibles and misdeeds. Many of us carefully selected our parents, and assigned ourselves the circumstances into which we were born. If the role is a humble one, we chose it in the belief that we could best atone for past errors by enduring hardships and surmounting difficult barriers. We felt that suffering was essential to the cleansing process. Therefore, it is not "who" we are in this brief lifetime, but "what" we think and do, and how cheerfully and lovingly we meet the challenges, that matters.

Why do most of us fail to remember our previous lives? Because the burden of such knowledge might be more than we could comfortably bear, and because a conscious awareness of old grievances, or former skills, could interfere with the new path that we have set out upon. Just as "the child is father of the man," so we are the sum total of all our attitudes, conduct and experiences in ages past. More importantly, we are busily creating the kind of person that we will become in the next lifetime, and the next.

If every man could accept the premise that he has no one except himself to blame for his misfortunes, and would resolve to atone for the error of his ways, the world could change dramatically. Warfare would disappear, for what person would dare to pursue the path of the aggressor? Who would rob, or kill, or rape if he were convinced that he was preparing a similar fate for himself? Race, sex, and religious prejudices would vanish if man knew that he himself had previously been, or in future would become, a Negro, an Oriental, a Catholic, a Jew, a Moslem, a Hindu, or a white woman. Rebellious youths could scarcely resent their parents if they thought that they had selected them in order to fulfill a particular mission for which they chose to be reborn; and parents might better understand their willful youngsters, knowing that they may previously have been their own father, sister, or formidable rival who wanted to be born to them to work out a karmic situation.

It is not overly important whether we "believe" in reincarnation. If the laws of karma and Grace are real, they will survive without our attestation. What does matter is that we conduct ourselves in such manner that we incur no bad karmic indebtedness. The skeptic may ask, "What if there's no such thing as karma, or reincarnation, or eternal life?"

Yes, but what if there is?